MW00436699

THE POPE'S LETTER AND SUNDAY LAW

Russell R. Standish B.A. (Honors), M.B., B.S. (Sydney University, Australia), M.R.C.P. (United Kingdom), F.R.C.P.(Edinburgh), F.R.C.P. (Glasgow)

Colin D. Standish, B.A. (Honors), M.A. (Honors), M.Ed., Ph.D. (Sydney University, Australia)

Published and Distributed by

**Hartland Publications
P.O. Box 1
Rapidan, VA 22733-0001**

Contents

Chapter I — The Pope's Letter

The Lord's Day — as Sunday was called from Apostolic Times." Thus commences Pope John Paul II's Apostolic Letter, *Dies Domini*, issued July 7, 1998. The Pope provides a reference in order to document his initial assertion. His reference is Revelation 1:10. This Scriptural passage states:

> I [John] was in the Spirit on the Lord's day, and heard behind me a great voice, as of a trumpet.

It will be seen that this verse of Scripture, while mentioning the Lord's Day, does not in any particular indicate which day of the week is the Lord's Day. One may read the context of the Biblical passage, and he will find no elucidation of the term. Since the term, "the Lord's Day" occurs nowhere else in Scripture, it will not assist us to seek another reference containing the term "Lord's Day" in order to enable us to discover the Biblical meaning of the term.

Yet the only safe ground for a sincere student of the Bible is to permit the Bible to interpret itself. God in His goodness has not left this matter in doubt. In clear, unequivocal terms He has revealed to us which day is the Lord's Day. The New Testament specifies the day which is the Lord's Day in two passages of Scripture:

For the Son of man is Lord even of the sabbath day (Matthew 12:8).

And he said unto them, That the Son of man is Lord also of the sabbath (Luke 6:5).

Plainly the Sabbath day *is* the Lord's Day. The Bible itself has cited this fact. But a new question arises: Which day is the Sabbath? The context of these two texts reveals that the Jews were accusing the disciples of sabbathbreaking in that they rubbed ears of corn in their hands. Clearly the day referred to was the day the Jews identified as the Sabbath.

If we are sincere searchers for Biblical truth, then we must permit the Scripture to identify the day which the Jews hallowed as the Sabbath. Once more the Bible is specific. Jesus was crucified on the day which many Christians designate as Good Friday. The Jews named that day the preparation day. Speaking of the day of Christ's death, Luke recorded:

And that day was the preparation, and the sabbath drew on (Luke 23:54).

Thus the Sabbath day of the Jews was the day after Friday.

This fact is confirmed in Matthew's account of the resurrection which occurred on the day many Christians, including Roman Catholics, uphold as Easter Sunday. Matthew repeated Mary Magdalene's visit to the empty tomb thus:

In the end of the sabbath, as it began to dawn toward the first day of the week, came Mary Magdalene and the other Mary to see the sepulchre (Matthew 28:1).

Manifestly the Sabbath day upon which the Jews worshipped was the day between Friday and Sunday. That day was Saturday.

Therefore, as we review Matthew 12:8 and Luke 6:5 quoted above, we are compelled to conclude that the Lord's Day, plainly identified in Scripture, is Saturday, the seventh day of the week. This causes no surprise, for the fourth commandment, written with God's own hand plainly states:

> Remember the sabbath day, to keep it holy. Six days shalt thou labour, and do all thy work: But *the seventh day is the sabbath of the Lord thy God:* in it thou shalt not do any work, thou, nor thy son, nor thy daughter, thy manservant, nor thy maidservant, nor thy cattle, nor thy stranger that is within thy gates: For in six days the Lord made heaven and earth, the sea, and all that in them is, and rested the seventh day: wherefore the Lord blessed the sabbath day, and hallowed it (Exodus 20:8-11, emphasis supplied).

So God, Himself, designated Saturday, the seventh day of the week, as the Lord's Day. Thus Revelation 1:10 is simply stating that John was in vision on the Sabbath, the seventh day of the week. The Bible, therefore, testifies that the Pope's initial statement is an incredible lapse from sound scholarship.

The initial statement in the Pope's Apostolic Letter also reveals a remarkable alteration in the position of the Roman Catholic stance on Sunday worship. Unlike some Protestants who have sought to uphold Sunday-sanctity on the basis of apostolic tradition, this has not been the practice of Roman Catholics. Let us review two authoritative statements of the Roman Catholic Church.

The first states:

> **Question** — Which is the Sabbath day? **Answer** — Saturday is the Sabbath day. **Question** — Why do we observe Sunday instead of Saturday? **Answer** — We observe Sunday instead of Saturday because the Catholic church, in the Council of Laodicea (364 A.D.) transferred the solemnity from Saturday to Sunday (Peter Geiermann [a Roman Catholic priest], *The Convert's Catechism of Catholic Doctrine,* second edition, p. 50).

The Roman Catholic Mirror emphatically discovered no Biblical evidence for the substitution of Sunday for Saturday for Sabbath observance.

> [We have] disposed of every text to be found in the New Testament referring to the Sabbath (Saturday), and to the first day of the week (Sunday); and [here] shown conclusively from these texts, that, so far, not a shadow of pretext can be found in the Sacred Volume for the Biblical substitution of Sunday for Saturday. Catholic Mirror, Sept. 16, 1893

Here we see that the Roman Catholic Church has long claimed that it altered the Sabbath from Saturday to Sunday in the year 336 A.D. That was certainly *not* apostolic times, as the Pope states in his Apostolic Letter. Almost two-and-a-half centuries had passed since the death of the last apostle until the Council of Laodicea convened. Millions of Roman Catholics have in their possession catechisms which assent that the *Council* altered the day of worship and not the apostles. These Catholics must be confused by the Pope's latest declaration on the matter. Strange indeed is this altered claim for a church which is reputed never to have changed.

A second catechism, approved by the Roman Catholic Church and authored by a priest, also raises questions concerning the commencement of the Pope's Apostolic Letter, for it would seem that the Pope is shrinking from the ecclesiastical authority which Roman Catholics have based upon the church's ability to alter the day of worship. This catechism states:

> **Question:** Do you have any other way of proving that the church has power to institute festivals and precepts? **Answer:** Had she not such power she could not have done that which all modern religionists agree with her, she could not have substituted the observance of Sunday the first day of the week, for the observance of Saturday, a change for which there is no Scriptural authority (Stephen Keenan, *A Doctrinal Catechism*).

Stephen Keenan correctly states that there is no Scriptural authority for Sunday observance. It would have been strange indeed if Sunday was the new Lord's Day and that not one of the eight authors of the New Testament stated this as a fact. It would have been an incredible oversight in the 260 chapters of the New Testament that no mention of such a dramatic alteration was provided.

Indeed, the author of Revelation, the apostle John, the only Bible writer to use the term, "the Lord's Day" (Revelation 1:10), mentioned Sunday twice in his gospel (John 20:1; 20:19). Both these verses refer to the day of Christ's resurrection. Surely if ever there was a time to call the first day of the week the Lord's Day, if it were appropriate, then this was the day. But John chose not to do so. Why? Because he well knew that the Lord's day was the Sabbath. Remember, John wrote his gospel between 80 – 90 A.D. If it had been his habit for 50 – 60 years after Jesus' death to address the Sunday as "the Lord's Day" he certainly would have used this term in his gospel.

In corroboration of *A Doctrinal Catechism,* The Catholic Mirror, which was the official Catholic newspaper of the Archdiocese of Baltimore, Maryland, USA, over which the eminent Cardinal Gibbons presided, stated,

> The Catholic Church for over one thousand years before the existence of a Protestant, by virtue of her divine mission, changed the day from Saturday to Sunday." (1893, p. 29)

In fact, a few Christians in the mid-second century had adopted the pagan day of the Roman Empire in order to escape confusion with Jews during periods of anti-Semitism in the Roman Empire. Justin Martyr in 155 was the first to mention this practice, but it was not a general practice in Christendom and was based upon fear of persecution, not Scriptural mandate.

The Catholic Mirror states its conclusion emphatically.

> Hence the conclusion is inevitable; viz., that of those who follow the Bible as their guide, the Israelites and Seventh-day Adventists, have the exclusive weight of evidence on their side, whilst the Biblical Protestant has not a word in self-defence for his substitution of Sunday for Saturday. *Catholic Mirror*, Sept. 9, 1893.

We must remember that every book of the New Testament was written decades after the death of Jesus. Eight times the first day of the week (Sunday) is mentioned (Matthew 28:1; Mark 16:2,9; Luke 24:1; John 20:1,19; Acts 20:7; 1 Corinthians 16:2). Not once is it referred to as the Lord's Day. Not once! The first six of these texts simply state that Christ rose from the dead on Sunday. The passage in 1 Corinthians merely admonishes the Christians to gather their offerings on Sunday.

Many Protestants, seeking to escape the Roman Catholic taunt that the acceptance of Sunday sacredness is an implied acceptance of the claimed papal authority to institute ecclesiastical festivals and precepts (laws) not found in Scripture, grasp at Acts 20:7 as the Biblical support of their Sunday worship.

Let us examine this passage of Scripture:

> And upon the first day of the week, when the disciples came together to break bread, Paul preached unto them, ready to depart on the morrow; and continued his speech until midnight (Acts 20:7).

There is no question that the believers met on Sunday. Unquestionably they "broke bread" on the Sunday. This fact has frequently been used as evidence that a communion service was held and thus Sunday must have been held sacred by Paul and the believers at Troas. This matter merits investigation.

Paul, the biblical record states, "continued his speech until midnight" (Acts 20:7). At about this time a tragedy occurred when a young man, Eutychus, fell asleep and fell from the window of the third loft and was killed (v. 9). Paul went downstairs and, through the power of God, Eutychus was restored to life (v. 10). Undoubtedly this procedure took some minutes, and it was the very early hours of the second day of the week (Monday) when Paul returned upstairs to the room where he had been preaching. It is pertinent to the matter under discussion to record that which occurred on that early Monday morning:

When he therefore was come up again, and had broken bread, and eaten, and talked a long while, even till break of day, so he departed (Acts 20: 11).

Thus Scripture testifies that Paul "had broken bread" on Monday morning. Yet no Christian uses this fact to support Monday sacredness. The fact that bread was broken also on Monday morning seriously diminishes the use of Acts 20:7 as evidence of Sunday sacredness.

But this is not all. What does the term "to break bread" mean? Once more Scripture comes to our aid as its own interpreter:

And they, continuing daily with one accord in the temple, and breaking bread from house to house, did eat their meat with gladness and singleness of heart (Acts 2:46).

Notice what this text reveals. Firstly, the early Christians, filled with the power of Pentecost, broke bread daily. So whatever the term "to break bread" meant, it provides absolutely no basis for selecting one of the seven days of the week as the special day of worship, for bread was broken on all days of the week.

Secondly, we have in this passage, clear evidence of the Biblical meaning of the term "to break bread." In other Scripture verses, this meaning includes the participation in the communion service. But plainly, this Scripture states, in qualifying this breaking of bread, that "they did eat their meat with gladness and singleness of heart." The word "meat" as used in the 17th and 18th centuries simply meant "food."

But there is yet another matter that requires our attention as we seek to understand this matter. If the day upon which the communion service was conducted indicated the timing of Sabbath observance, then surely we would follow Christ's example and keep holy the day on which He instituted this ordinance. Since the first Lord's Supper was held on the evening before Christ's crucifixion, such a concept would lead us to observe Thursday as our day of worship. No Christian follows such an absurdity.

Thus Acts 20:7 as a valid support for Sunday sacredness falls on three counts — 1) the breaking of bread was a daily matter; 2) the Scriptural meaning of the term was to enjoy a meal; and 3) Christ instituted the Lord's Supper on a Thursday evening. In citing these three irrefutable facts, we have not mentioned that the Jewish day commenced, not at midnight, but at sunset. Thus long before midnight, by Jewish (and Scriptural) reckoning, Paul had been preaching on the second day of the week, Monday. Manifestly, the use of Acts 20:7 does not present a strong case for Sunday sacredness and, indeed, is quite invalid as a Scriptural argument for Sunday observance.*

Once more, we would remind each reader that at no time do the Biblical writers refer to the first day of the week as the Lord's Day. Constantly they refer to the Sabbath, never once referring to it as the former Sabbath or in any other way indicating that the seventh day of the week no longer held validity as God's holy day. That would be remarkable if Christ's death altered His law since, as we have stated, every book of the New Testament was written decades after Christ's death. Indeed, the seventh-day Sabbath is mentioned in the New Testament no less than 60 times.

In the second paragraph of his Apostolic Letter, the Pope further makes an assertion which no doubt has proven puzzling to many readers. He states,

---

*   We have assumed that Luke, the author of the book Acts of the Apostles, was using the Roman reckoning of time rather than the Jewish. The Bible is not clear on whether this episode in the book Acts of the Apostles was using Jewish or Roman time. The Jews commenced each new day at sunset and the Romans commenced it at midnight.

    Three matters inclined us to believe that this meetings occurred on Sunday evening, not Saturday evening as it would have been had the reference been based on the Jewish mode of reckoning days.

1. Luke would have been raised with the Roman form of dividing days. He was the author of the book of Acts.
2. Even John, who was a Jew, used the Roman method of reckoning. The evening he mentioned as the first day of the week could not have been Saturday evening, as Christ had not yet risen from the dead.

    "Then the same day at evening, being the first *day* of the week, when the doors were

Rightly, then, the Psalmist's cry is applied to Sunday: ' This is the day which the Lord has made: let us rejoice and be glad in it' (Psalms 118:24).

Children still in elementary school, if raised in a Christian or Jewish home, will know that the Jewish nation observed Saturday, the seventh day specified in God's Law, as their sacred day. There can be no question whatsoever that the psalmist in this verse of his ancient Hebrew hymn is referring to Saturday. This passage can in no way be rightly applied to Sunday. To do so is to wrest the Scriptures.

Thus the Apostolic Letter, *Dies Domini,* commences in such a fashion that one is left questioning the care with which it has been prepared. This is the more surprising when we consider that there is no doubt whatsoever that some of the highest intellects in the Roman Catholic Church and in the Vatican would have assisted the Pope in the preparation of this letter.

This matter is not ameliorated by the fact that in his fifth paragraph, the Pope makes another false claim. He states that "the fundamental importance of Sunday has been recognized through two thousand years of history." If, as *The Convert's Catechism of Catholic Doctrine* asserts, the Catholic church, in the Council of Laodicea (336 A.D.) transferred the solemnity from Saturday to Sunday then the very longest period Sunday has been recognized as the Sabbath is 1663 years (at the date of publication of this book). Even this period

---

shut where the disciples were assembled for fear of the Jews, came Jesus and stood in the midst, and saith unto them, Peace *be* unto you." (John 20:19)

3. The Bible plainly states that when Paul preached on the evening of the first day of the week he planned to sail "on the morrow." If the Jewish reckoning was in use, then Paul would have been sailing not on the morrow but later the same day. (See Acts 20:7).

However, if it were Saturday evening to which Luke referenced as would be so if the Jewish commencement of the day was here indicated, then it would have been Saturday evening and not Sunday upon which those gathered initially broke bread. This would provide absolutely no basis for the use of this passage of Scripture as a Biblical mandate for Sunday worship, for Saturday evening is most certainly not a portion of the present Sunday which commences at midnight.

is confined largely to the Roman Catholic Church. As Benjamin Wilkinson, in his classic work, *Truth Triumphant,* documents, the seventh-day Sabbath was upheld in Scotland until 1206, in India until the 16th century, Ethiopia until the 17th century, in Eastern Europe until the 16th century, and in China at least to the 14th century.

In 1956, the book, *The Faith of Millions* was published and sold in Catholic bookstores. It asserted (page 473) that

...since Saturday, and not Sunday, is specified in the Bible, isn't it curious that non-Catholics who profess to take their religion directly from the Bible and not from the church, observe Sunday instead of Saturday.

In December 1893, the eminent American Cardinal, Archbishop Gibbons, asserted that there were just two alternatives in this matter. Either one accepts the Bible as the basis of one's faith, a position accepted by Protestantism, and thus keep Saturday holy, or accept the Catholic dogma of the authority of the church, and thus worship on Sunday.

Cardinal Gibbons' claim is valid. Numerous Protestant authorities concur that Saturday is the true Sabbath and that there is no apostolic or Biblical basis for Sunday observance. It is prudent that we document a selection of these sources. Emphasis supplied.

There was and is a commandment to keep holy the Sabbath day, but that Sabbath Day was not Sunday. It will be said, however, and with some show of triumph, that the Sabbath was transferred from the seventh to the first day of the week....Where can the record of such a transaction be found? Not in the New Testament — absolutely not....Of course, I quite well know that Sunday did come into use in early Christian history as a religious day, as we learn from the Christian Fathers, and other sources. But WHAT A PITY that it comes branded with the mark of paganism, and christened with the name of the sun god, when adopted and sanctioned by the papal apostasy, and bequeathed as a sacred legacy to Protestantism! — Dr. Edward T. Hiscox *(author of the Baptist Manual), Source Book,* pp. 513,514.

Centuries of the Christian era passed away before Sunday was observed by the Christian church as the Sabbath. History does not furnish us with a SINGLE PROOF or INDICATION that it was AT ANY TIME so observed previous to the Sabbatical edict of Constantine in 321 A.D. — Sir William Domville, of the Church of England, *The Sabbath or An Examination of the Six Texts*, p. 291.

So some have tried to build the observance of Sunday upon apostolic command, whereas the apostles gave no command on the matter....The truth is, as soon as we appeal to the 'Litera scripta' (the literal writing) of the Bible, the Sabbatarians have the best of the argument. — *The Presbyterian At Work*, editorial, April 19, 1883.

It is true, there is no positive command for infant baptism...nor is there any for keeping the first day of the week. — The Methodist Theological Compendium.

It is quite clear that however rigidly or devotedly we may spend Sunday, we are not keeping the Sabbath. The Sabbath was founded on a specific, divine command. We can plead no such command for the observance of Sunday....There is not a single line in the New Testament to suggest that we incur any penalty by violating the supposed sanctity of Sunday. — Dr. W. R. Dale (Congregational), *The Ten Commandments*, pp. 106,107.

The observance of the Lord's day (Sunday) is founded not on any command of God, but on the authority of the church. — Augsburg Confession of Faith (Lutheran).

The festival of Sunday, like all other festivals, was always only a human ordinance, and it was far from the intentions of the apostles to establish a divine command in this respect, far from them and from the early apostolic church to transfer the laws of the Sabbath to Sunday. — Johann Neander (Episcopalian), *General History of the Christian Religion and Church*, p. 186.

Why then has the Pope adopted a novel approach in attempting to vindicate Sunday observance, not from church authority, but rather from Scripture? Only he and perhaps his inner circle of counselors could explain this remarkable alteration of course. It surely is unnecessary for faithful Roman Catholics. They have already accepted papal authority to alter and enact ecclesiastical festivals and laws, without Scriptural warrant. Perhaps the Pope sees in the increasing clamor for Sunday laws amongst Evangelical Protestants, that now is the time to woo them to his cause by presenting his call for similar laws upon grounds which will appeal to these Protestants by claiming to appeal to holy writ.

Whatever the Pope's motive is, he has placed his own church in a frightful dilemma. Only time will tell how he or his successor will attempt to extricate the Roman Catholic Church from this self-created quandary.

While ever the Papacy asserted the fact that the seventh-day Sabbath was observed in apostolic times, and that this practice continued even in the western Christian Church until the fourth century, it was possible to claim papal authority for the church's alteration. Sunday worship was declared to be the mark of that authority. By appealing to Scripture and apostolic practice, the Pope has forfeited that claimed authority and vested that authority in Scripture. But since Scripture does not support his claim, he has led the Roman Catholic Church into a theological quagmire. As numerous Roman Catholic leaders have correctly claimed, there is no Biblical basis for Sunday observance, absolutely none! Therefore the Pope has placed the sacred observance of Sunday upon an extremely weak platform. He has opened a door to demonstrate the vulnerability of the Christian churches' position on this matter, for in truth, Sunday observance, as the author of the *Baptist Manual,* Dr. Edward Hiscox, stated, is based upon no better principle than

> ...it comes branded with the mark of paganism, christened with the name of the sun god, when adopted and sanctioned by papal apostasy, and bequeathed as a sacred legacy to Protestantism (*Source Book,* p. 514).

While scattered instances of Christians worshipping on the pagan day of the sun in order to escape persecution engineered by the mistaken concept that they were Jewish have been documented, Sabbathkeeping was generally upheld until the conversion of Constantine, Emperor of the Roman Empire in 321 A.D. The depth of his conversion from paganism is not for us to judge. Suffice it to record that he advocated, after his conversion, that the day of the sun, Sunday, be observed.

The Pope cannot simultaneously hold two mutually exclusive positions. Sunday sanctity has for centuries been the pillar of the Roman Catholic Church's claim to ecclesiastical authority. This claim has ever been based upon the fact that the Bible contains no mandate for Sunday observance. It has been Rome's stated position that

> had she no such power, she could not have done that in which all modern religionists agree with her, she could not have substituted the observance of Sunday, the first day of the week, for the observance of Saturday, a change for which there is no Scriptural authority (Stephen Keenan, *A Doctrinal Catechism).*

Either the Papacy has to renounce its usurped ecclesiastical authority and support its new claim to discover a Biblical basis for Sunday observance, or it must continue to assert its supreme authority in matters ecclesiastical and admit that Sunday worship is its own invention, devoid of Scriptural confirmation.

As we have demonstrated, the Pope's Apostolic Letter provides a faulted introduction to his new approach, and the remainder of the letter fares no better.

If the Roman Catholic Church resorts to its former position that Scripture provides no basis for Sunday observance and that it was not practiced or advocated in apostolic times, then the man it claims to be its first pontiff, the apostle Peter, did not share the practice nor exert the authority usurped by subsequent popes.

The Apostolic Letter, *Dies Domini,* has placed the Roman Catholic Church in a most difficult position.

Chapter 2 — The Implications of Sunday Legislation

The Pope in his Apostolic Letter, *Dies Domini*, dated May 31, 1998, but released on July 7, 1998, introduced a matter which was both disturbing and of the utmost importance. Ponder John Paul's words:

> Therefore, also in the particular circumstances of our own time, Christians will naturally strive to ensure that civil legislation respects their duty to keep Sunday holy.

Civil legislation? Civil legislation has only one place, and one place alone, in matters of religion and personal conviction. That prerogative is to guarantee full religious liberty and free practice of faith to all citizens of the nation. Of course, vile crimes such as human sacrifice must not be encompassed by such liberty. But care must be taken not to extend such exceptions beyond the realm of criminal acts abhorrent to mankind.

If the Pope in this matter is making a plea for civil legislation to guarantee full religious liberty for all citizens to practice their faith, we applaud it. If he is asserting the right of man to refrain from taking part in all aspects of religion, we could not rightly take issue with this plea. But this does not appear to be the intent of John Paul's words.

Three paragraphs prior to the statement quoted above, the Pope, of course in a manner designed to limit the serious implications of that which he has suggested, speaks of his church having enacted Sunday laws in times past. The historical record of such church laws is far from exemplary, for coercion rather than liberty was the hallmark of such legislation. The Pope speaks of the church laws being enacted, having "in mind above all the work of servants and workers." He further reminded his readers that

Pope Leo XIII in his Encyclical *Rerum Novarum* spoke of Sunday rest as a worker's right which the State must guarantee.

There is no provision in Leo XIII's Encyclical for workers' rights in the matter of seventh-day Sabbath observance, should that be their convictions.

Our concerns are increased when we take regard of a previous Apostolic Letter issued by the Pope on May 28, 1998. In this Apostolic Letter, *Ad Tuendam Fidem* (To Protect the Faith), which was designed to insert new codes into Canon Law, the new Canon 1436 is a cause for grave concern. It states:

Canon 1436 – § 1. Whoever denies a truth which must be believed with divine and catholic faith, or who calls into doubt, or who totally repudiates the Christian faith, and does not retract after having been legitimately warned, is to be punished as a heretic or an apostate with a major excommunication; a cleric moreover can be punished with other penalties, not excluding deposition.

§ 2. In addition to these cases, whoever obstinately rejects a teaching that the Roman Pontiff or the College of Bishops, exercising the authentic Magisterium, have set forth to be held definitively, or who affirms what they have condemned as erroneous, and does not retract after having been legitimately warned, is to be punished with an appropriate penalty.

Here "punishment as a heretic" is invoked, together with a mystifying "punishment with an appropriate penalty." With such ill-defined punishment we could be forgiven if we reflected upon the history of the Inquisition. Peter de Rosa, a former professor of theology at Corpus Christi College and Professor of Ethics at Westminster Seminary, both Roman Catholic institutions, in his book, *Vicars of Christ,* (Corgi Books, 1989, London, p. 244) stated that 80 successive popes implemented the Inquisition.

In his Apostolic Letter, *Dies Domini,* John Paul II appealed to Pope Leo XIII, who reigned from 1878–1903. John Paul wrote,

> My predecessor, Pope Leo XIII in his Encyclical *Rerum Novarum* spoke of Sunday rest as a worker's right which the State must guarantee.

The appeal to Leo XIII is of concern. It will be noted that he, too, called upon the State, the civil authorities, to support Sunday sacredness. Further, Leo XIII was no friend of religious liberty. He officially declared in his Papal Encyclical on Human Liberty,

> Let us examine that liberty in individuals which is so opposed to the virtue of religion, namely the liberty of worship, as it is called. This is based on the principle that every man is free to profess as he may choose any religion or none....A liberty such as we have described...is no liberty, but is degradation (The Great Encyclical Letters of Pope Leo XIII, 3rd addition, Benzinger, 1903, pp. 149, 150).

Leo XIII's predecessor, Pope Pius IX, who held the papal seat longer than any pope in history (1846–1878), held identical views of religious liberty. In his *Syllabus of Errors,* issued December 8, 1864, Pope Pius IX condemned 80 matters which he listed as "errors". Two are worthy of record in respect of the matter of religious liberty.

> No. 15 Every man is free to embrace or profess that religion which, guided by the light of reason, he shall consider true.

> No. 24 The church has not the power of force, nor has she any

temporal power, direct or indirect.

Again we emphasize that Pius IX declared these matters, upholding religious liberty and precluding the church from the use of temporal force, to be errors.

Such a philosophy of freedom leaves wide open the door of punishment for simply holding convictions contrary to those of the Roman Catholic Church, even when the individual leads an exemplary life as a citizen in all respects. It is surely the thinking of the Dark Ages, not the nineteenth century.

The Roman Catholic Church has a long track record of what it considers as appropriate and just punishment for heretics. Estimates of the number who died at the hand of the Church range from 50 million to 120 million.

The revered Roman Catholic saint and theologian, Thomas Aquinas, wrote,

> With regard to heretics…on their own side there is sin, by which they deserve not only to be separated from the church by excommunication, but also to be severed from the world by death. *(SUMMA THEOLOGICA* Part II of second part, question 11, article 3, Vol. 2 page 440).

The cruelties of the Inquisition are too horrible to recount, yet modern scholars have for several decades been reappraising the Inquisition.

> Some now maintain the justice meted out, although brutal, was neither capricious nor unusual for the times. (*Courier Mail*, Brisbane, Australia, Nov. 2, 1998).

This is a most disconcerting assessment since it was largely the papacy which fashioned those times.

The *Libro Nero* (Black Book), a guide to Inquisitors, which was still on display in the Vatican last century, typifies papal justice, especially as many confessions were not made because of guilt but in order to spare the accused further cruel torture. The Inquisitors were admonished,

> Either the person confesses and he is proved guilty from his own confession, or he does not confess and is equally guilty on the evidence of witnesses (many of whom were unreliable). If a person confesses the whole of what he is accused of, he is unquestionably guilty of the whole; but if he confesses only a part, he ought still be regarded as guilty of the whole, since what he has confessed proves him to be capable of guilt as to the other points of accusation (Peter de Rosa, *Vicars of Christ,* p. 228, Corgi Books, London, 1989).

That death of heretics was still regarded as appropriate in the early part of the twentieth century is evidenced in a book written by Dr. Mariano de Luca in 1901. This book was based upon a series of lectures which Dr. de Luca had presented. The book contains a letter from Pope Leo XIII highly commending Dr. de Luca's presentations. Dr. de Luca quoted,

> The civil magistrate, by the command and commission of the church, ought to punish the heretic with the penalty of death. (Institutions of Ecclesiastical Public Law, p. 261). NOTE: The statement is a quote from Dr. Tanner positively presented by Dr. de Luca.

In 1910, Alexis Lépicier, professor of Sacred Theology in the Pontifical Urban College of Propaganda in Rome, reiterated the claim that the state should inflict death on heretics (*On the Stability and Progress of Dogma*, 2nd edition, pp. 194–210).

Thus, Pope John Paul II's enactment of new punitive laws for heretics is no trivial threat to the welfare and liberties of mankind. Since his apostolic letter *Ad Tuendum Fidem* includes all Christians, it is a great challenge as Protestantism moves rapidly towards Rome. The introduction states:

> To protect the faith of the Catholic Church against errors arising from certain members of the *Christian* faithful. (Emphasis added)

The significance should not be lost upon the reader, if a non-Catholic, that the new canon law 1436 was addressed to "Whoever" and the new canon law 1371 was directed to "a person who...." Thus they are not confined to Roman Catholic adherents.

While the Pope may not be considering such extreme penalties, nevertheless the vague nature of the penalties provides an open-ended decision-making process. Thus Canon 1436 speaks of "an appropriate penalty" while the other new Canon, 1371, refers to punishment for lack of doctrinal orthodoxy to be meted out with a "just penalty." Such lack of specificity was that which opened the way to imprisonment and death in ages past.

Of course many would claim that times have so changed since the period of the Inquisition that such would never be tolerated. But the Bible plainly declares that just prior to Christ's coming both economic boycotts and death will be imposed upon faithful followers of Christ, simply because their convictions are at odds with the majority faith. Christ, Himself, warned,

> They shall put you out of the synagogues; yea, the time cometh, that whosoever killeth you will think that he doeth God service (John 16:2).

In the book of the end-time Jesus plainly stated the final events of earth's history. Remember that this book is the revelation of Jesus Christ (Revelation 1:1).

> And deceiveth them that dwell on the earth by the means of those miracles which he had power to do in the sight of the beast, saying to them that dwell on the earth, that they should make an image to the beast, which had the wound by a sword and did live. And he had power to give life unto the image of the beast, that the image should both speak, and cause that as many as would not worship the image of the beast should be killed. And he causeth all, both small and great, rich and poor, free and bond, to receive a mark in their right hand, or in their foreheads: And that no man might buy or sell, save he that had the mark, or the name of the beast, or the number of his name (Revelation 13: 14-17).

To many, the language of this passage may seem initially incomprehensible. But the 13th chapter of Revelation provides ample evidence to make this passage all too plain. This we shall see. But firstly let us extract the plain matters in the quoted passage:

1. This is an issue of worship (verse 15).

2. Massive deception will be perpetrated upon the entire world (verse 16).

3. The central focus is a "beast which had a wound by a sword and did live" (verse 14).

4. A mark will be received by those who accept the worship of this coercive power (verses 16, 17).

5. There will be an economic boycott of dissenters (verse 17).

6. There will be a death sentence for dissenters (verse 15).

7. There is a "he" who will empower "the beast" and assist the "beast" in the prosecution of dissenters (verse 15).

We need to identify several matters from the above facts. Having done so, this issue will be perfectly clear. These matters are:

1. The identity of "the beast which had the wound."

2. The mysterious "mark" which will save people from both the economic boycott and the universal death decree.

3. The "he" who has so much worldwide influence that "he" can enforce economic boycotts and death decrees worldwide in support of the "beast's" form of worship.

Let us first identify the "mark." The Bible identifies this "mark" in other passages of Scripture. Whatever it is, it is a most telling and important matter. As we have seen in the above passage, it is of such value that the possessors of it, whether in the forehead or in the right hand, will be spared both severe economic sanctions and execution.

But further investigation of the mark of this "beast" power reveals that it is a double-sided coin. On the other side it provides the most dire penalties from God for those who possess this mark. Let us look at those Scriptural passages which plainly declare this fact.

> And the third angel followed them, saying with a loud voice, *If any man worship the beast and his image, and receive his mark in his forehead, or in his hand*, The same shall drink of the wine of the wrath of God, which is poured out without mixture into the cup of his indignation; and he shall be tormented with fire and brimstone in the presence of the holy angels, and in the presence of the Lamb: And the smoke of their torment ascendeth up for ever and ever: and they have no rest day nor night, who worship the beast and his image, and whosoever *receiveth the mark of his name* (Revelation 14:9-11).

This passage of Scripture reveals:

1. That this is an issue of worship (verse 9,11).

2. That the bearers of "the mark" will reap the awesome wrath of God (verse 10,11).

> And I heard a great voice out of the temple saying to the seven angels, Go your ways, and pour out the vials of the wrath of God upon the earth. And the first went, and poured out his vial upon the earth; and there fell a noisome and grievous sore upon the men which had the mark of the beast, and upon them which worshipped his image (Revelation 16:1,2).

These verses reveal that those who receive "the mark of the beast" will be the recipients of the seven last plagues — plagues of a magnitude never previously known upon earth. (For details of each of the seven plagues read the entire chapter of Revelation 16.)

> And the beast was taken, and with him the false prophet that wrought miracles before him, with which he deceived them that had received the mark of the beast, and them that worshipped his image. These

both were cast alive into a lake of fire burning with brimstone (Revelation 19:20).

The third of this trilogy of passages instructs us as follows:

1. The "beast" and the "he" ("the false prophet that wrought miracles — compare with Revelation 13:14 — those who accepted the mark) will be destroyed in the final conflagration.

2. Again the issue of worship is emphasized — "worshipped his image." Thus worship is a key issue in this matter of "the mark."

3. Those who receive "the mark" will also be destroyed in the final destruction of the wicked.

    And to you who are troubled rest with us, when the Lord Jesus shall be revealed from heaven with his mighty angels, In flaming fire taking vengeance on them that obey not the gospel of our Lord Jesus Christ: Who shall be punished with everlasting destruction from the presence of the Lord, and from the glory of his power (2 Thessalonians 1: 7-9).

Clearly then, at the end of earth's history mankind will be required to make a choice. This is no easy choice. Those who accept the mark of the beast will be spared the economic boycotts and execution to be meted out to the small group which refrains from enforced worship. On the other hand, they will incur the wrath of God and will suffer the seven last plagues and eternal destruction in the final conflagration.

This coerced worship will be almost universal.

    And all that dwell upon the earth shall worship him, whose names are not written in the book of life of the Lamb slain from the foundation of the world" (Revelation 13:8).

This fact should provide every Christian pause to consider the final goals of the ecumenical movement. While it is true that Christ prayed for unity amongst Christians (John 17:21), it was not unity based upon compromise and/or error. Christ never taught unity at any price. Notice that the prayer for unity recorded in John 17:21 is based upon Christ's platform of truth.

> Sanctify them through thy truth: thy word is truth.... And for their sakes I sanctify myself, that they also might be sanctified through the truth (John 17:17, 19).

The ecumenical movement de-emphasizes truth and doctrinal convictions in order to obtain uniformity amongst the members of churches which holds doctrines which are diametrically opposed. Let us illustrate. Presbyterians believe in predestination. On the other hand, Methodists believe in free choice. Episcopalians believe in infant baptism. Baptists practice adult believer baptism. The Salvation Army has no form of baptism, nor do they engage in the communion service, unlike most other faiths. Some segments of the Church of England practice confession to priests, while the Lutherans confess directly to Christ. The Eastern Orthodox churches utilize icons and images in their worship, while the Church of the Nazarenes does not. The Church of Christ eschews the use of musical instruments in its services, while most other faiths utilize such instruments. Some faiths assert the doctrine of once saved, always saved; others believe that salvation is conditioned upon continual obedience. Doctrinal positions, such as the immortality of the soul and its opposite, the belief in death as a "sleep," have to be submerged in the ecumenical movement. So too do the doctrinal views of the earthly millennium and its converse, the millennium in heaven. The difference between Sunday, as opposed to Saturday sanctity has to be submerged if the ecumenical movement is to succeed in its aims.

That it will all but succeed is made evident in the prophecy of Revelation 13:8 quoted above. However, the context of this Scripture informs us that this move for a single world religion is far from God's choosing and is inimical to salvation, for the minority clearly are the ones whose names are written in the Book of Life and thus receive salvation. The great majority will forfeit salvation. This confirms Isaiah's prophecy (Isaiah 10: 22, 23) which Paul applied to the Christian Church.

> Esaias also crieth concerning Israel, Though the number of the children of Israel be as the sand of the sea, a remnant shall be saved" (Romans 9:27).

Every devout Christian should reevaluate the aims of the ecumenical movement. Manifestly it is not designed of God.

It will be this remnant featured in the prophecies of Isaiah and Romans who will be saved. Those are the very same people who refuse to accept the mark of the beast. Speaking of such people, when redeemed in heaven, we are informed,

> And I saw as it were a sea of glass mingled with fire: and them that had gotten the victory over the beast, and over his image, and over his mark, and over the number of his name, stand on the sea of glass, having the harps of God. And they sing the song of Moses the servant of God, and the song of the Lamb, saying, Great and marvellous *are* thy works, Lord God Almighty; just and true *are* thy ways, thou King of saints (Revelation 15:2, 3).

Chapter 3 — The Seal of God and The Mark of the Beast

It is imperative that we identify the mark of the beast, for our salvation depends upon our rejection of this mark. So let us first seek the identifying characteristics of those who compose this remnant which will receive the great joy of salvation. The prophet Zephaniah plainly identifies the remnant. They are believers who possess three character traits.

> The remnant of Israel shall not do iniquity, nor speak lies, neither shall a deceitful tongue be found in their mouth (Zephaniah 3:13).

These people of the remnant thus possess the following characteristics:

1. They do no iniquity (in God's strength, yielding to Him day by day and moment by moment they have confessed and forsaken their sins).

2. They speak no lies.

3. They possess no deceitful tongue.

Characteristics 2 and 3 are allied. The term "guile" is a single word incorporating lying with deceit.

It is of no small import that these two characteristics are the precise characteristics cited as a summary of Christ's character.

> For even hereunto were ye called: because Christ also suffered for us, leaving us an example, that ye should follow his steps: Who did no sin, neither was guile found in his mouth (1 Peter 2:21, 22).

It is vital that we ponder this passage, for here all Christians are admonished to seek God's power, which is sent through the Holy Spirit, in order to emulate Christ's character. Notice Christ's character was summarized as possessing two features —

1. He did no sin.

2. There was no guile in His mouth.

Thus the remnant of Zephaniah 3:13 are those who have followed Christ's example in His character. Yet today many members of the clergy make no calls for their flock to earnestly seek, through prayer, the faith which will provide them with the power of the Holy Spirit to develop characters akin to that of Jesus. Of even greater concern is the fact that not a few shepherds of the flock encourage their members to believe that consistent sin in the life is no barrier to salvation. Those who accept such unscriptural error will receive the mark of the beast for they are clearly unqualified to be a portion of the remnant who shall be saved.

> Esaias also crieth concerning Israel, Though the number of the children of Israel be as the sand of the sea, a remnant shall be saved (Romans 9:27).

Some may cry, "Legalism"! No! A thousand times, No! To reflect Christ's character is simply to love Him tenderly and wholeheartedly.

> If ye love me, keep my commandments (John 14:15).

Further, let us notice what Scripture attests concerning the end-time saints. It is not without great significance that the words immediately following Christ's severe denunciation of those who receive the mark of the beast are as follows:

> Here is the patience of the saints: here are they that keep the commandments of God, and have the faith of Jesus (Revelation 14:12).

The question rightly arises, Are we not saved by grace (God's mercy), and grace alone? The answer to this question is an emphatic Yes! Scripture testifies to this fact.

> For by grace are ye saved through faith; and that not of yourselves: it is the gift of God: not of works, lest any man should boast (Ephesians 2:8, 9).

Thus even the possession of a Christ-like character provides no ground or basis for our salvation. Christ's immeasurable grace, His mercy, alone saves us from our sins. This fact must never be minimized. It is a central gospel fact. That grace is provided for us through the death of our Saviour on Calvary. We are not saved by the development of a Christ-like character. But, we cannot be saved without it, for the possession of such a character, as we have seen, is an inevitable result of partaking of God's grace.

So important is this truth that Christ impressed it on the tables of stone when preparing His ten commandments. Unfortunately the Roman Catholic Church has deigned to entirely expunge this matter from the ten commandments. God wrote,

> And shewing mercy unto thousands of them that love me, and keep my commandments (Exodus 20:6).

God's mercy in providing salvation, that is, His saving grace, is not bestowed without conditions. These conditions are love for Him and keeping His commandments. This passage of Scripture, while present in Roman Catholic versions of Scripture such as the Douay

Version, and the Jerusalem Bible, has been removed from Roman Catholic catechisms, as has the remainder of the second commandment.

> Thou shalt not make unto thee any graven image, or any likeness of any thing that is in heaven above, or that is in the earth beneath, or that is in the water under the earth: Thou shalt not bow down thyself to them, nor serve them: for I the Lord thy God am a jealous God, visiting the iniquity of the fathers upon the children unto the third and fourth generation of them that hate me; And shewing mercy unto thousands of them that love me, and keep my commandments (Exodus 20:4-6).

Keep this in mind as we further evaluate the meaning of the mark of the beast. Those who have read John Paul's Apostolic Letter and have been confused by his continual reference to the Sabbath commandment as the third commandment need to understand that the Roman Catholic Church's expulsion of the second commandment from the decalogue necessitates the altering of the numeration of the ten commandments. Thus Roman Catholics refer to the Sabbath commandment as the third and not the fourth, as Scripture testifies.

The Bible teaches that the entire ground for our salvation is grace, while the condition upon which grace is bestowed is faith that is manifested in obedience to God's commandments (Eph. 2:8, James 2:9,10), an obedience found in God's last-day saints (Revelation 14:12). Scripture even asserts that it is the remnant who keep God's commandments, upon whom the dragon, who in Revelation 12:9 is identified as Satan, focuses his great rage in the last days of earth's history (Revelation 12:17).

We have seen that the remnant will possess the character of Christ which is summarized in 1 Peter 2:22 by two features — He did no sin, and no guile was found in His mouth. But there is another very important group at the end of time which will possess this same character. Indeed, this group of faithful people, called by another name, are identical to the remnant. They are crucial to our discovery of the nature of the mark of the beast.

This synonym for the remnant is the 144,000. Listen to the summary of their characters.

And in their mouth was found no guile: for they are without fault before the throne of God (Revelation 14:5).

We see that they share with Christ mouths without guile, and are faultless (sinless) before the throne of God. God declares,

I will not justify the wicked (Exodus 23:7).

Of course, the remnant/144,000, are redeemed sinners, for all have sinned (Romans 3:23). But in the power of the Holy Spirit they have developed a life of overcoming.

This is a characteristic of genuine belief. Many Christians accept two statements of Scripture with no better belief than do Satan and his angels. Let it not be forgotten that

the devils also believe and tremble (James 2:19).

But this intellectual acknowledgment alone is Satan's counterfeit version of belief. Be not deceived, Satan has counterfeited every virtue of God.

Yet Scripture does assent

that whosoever believeth in him should not perish, but have eternal life. For God so loved the world, that he gave his only-begotten Son, that whosoever believeth in him should not perish, but have everlasting life (John 3:15, 16).

Here Christ guaranteed eternal life on the condition of belief. Paul and Silas gave the same assurance to the jailer.

And they said, Believe on the Lord Jesus Christ and thou shalt be saved, and thy house (Acts 16:31).

So then in what way does genuine belief differ from the belief that Satan and his angels possess, and that which he offers as a deceptive substitute for the genuine? The following passage presents the features of true belief in Christ.

> Whosoever believeth that Jesus is the Christ is born of God: and every one that loveth him that begat loveth him also that is begotten of him. By this we know that we love the children of God, when we love God, and keep his commandments. For this is the love of God, that we keep his commandments: and his commandments are not grievous. For whatsoever is born of God overcometh the world: and this is the victory that overcometh the world, even our faith. Who is he that overcometh the world, but he that believeth that Jesus is the Son of God? (1 John 5:1-5).

Take note that this entire passage is related to genuine belief, for this fact is stated in the first and the last verses of the passage.

Now let us highlight the seven character features of true belief enumerated in this passage of God's Word:

1. We must be born of God — the new birth experience (verses 1,4).

2. We love our neighbor as ourselves (verses 1,2).

3. We love God with the whole heart (verses 1,2,3).

4. We keep (obey) God's commandments (verses 2,3).

5. We must overcome the world/worldliness (verses 4,5).

6. We must have victory over sin (verse 4).

7. We must have faith, the faith of Jesus (verse 4).

Few Christians who describe themselves as "believers" measure up to these criteria. The five foolish virgins were "believers," but because they lacked the oil in their lamps, the symbol of the Holy Spirit and His power in their lives, they failed to attain eternal life for they had accepted the devil's counterfeit belief.

The same is true of the Christians described by Christ, who will be aghast that they have failed to gain eternal life.

> Not every man that saith unto me, Lord, Lord, shall enter into the kingdom of heaven: but he that doeth the will of my Father which is in heaven. Many will say to me in that day, Lord, Lord, have we not prophesied in thy name? and in thy name have cast out devils? and in thy name done many wonderful works? And then will I profess unto them, I never knew you: depart from me, ye that work iniquity (Matthew 7:21-23).

We observe that these "believers" did many works, but they did not possess the character of Christ for they did not do the will of God. Many of these have been beguiled by preachers who have promised salvation to those who neglect to meet the conditions. The remnant/144,000 have not accepted such sophistries.

Let us now return to the 144,000, for it is they who enlighten our understanding of the mark of the beast. The redeemed are first mentioned by this designation as follows:

> And I saw another angel ascending from the east, having the seal of the living God: and he cried with a loud voice to the four angels, to whom it was given to hurt the earth and the sea, Saying, Hurt not the earth, neither the sea, nor the trees, till we have sealed the servants of our God in their foreheads. And I heard the number of them which were sealed: *and there were* sealed an hundred *and* forty *and* four thousand of all the tribes of the children of Israel. (Revelation 7:2–4).

Some have interpreted this group as being composed solely of Jews. No doubt it will include faithful Jews who have accepted Christ, but other details of this group and the fact that they are synonymous with the remnant excludes the view that the 144,000 is entirely composed of ethnic Jews. This passage must be understood in the New Testament usage of the term "Israel" or "Abraham's seed."

> And if ye be Christ's, then are ye Abraham's seed, and heirs according to the promise (Galatians 3:29).

Revelation 7:2,3 reveals that prior to the release of the winds of strife which will lead to the seven last plagues, the 144,000 will receive the seal of the living God in their foreheads. Bear in mind that the mark of the beast is also placed in the forehead, but in addition it may be received in the right hand (Revelation 13:16). We have documented from scripture that those who receive the mark of the beast compose the lost. We shall see that those who receive the seal of the living God are the redeemed. Thus if we can elucidate the meaning of the seal of the living God, we will in no wise be in difficulty in understanding the nature of the mark of the beast.

The seal of the living God represents character. This is evidenced by Scripture for the seal of the living God is described as follows:

And I looked, and, lo, a Lamb stood on the mount Sion, and with him an hundred forty and four thousand, having his Father's name written in their foreheads (Revelation 14:1).

The seal of God thus is the Father's name inscribed in the forehead. What does this mean? God's name represents His character. In the Lord's prayer we are encouraged to pray

Hallowed be thy name (Matthew 6:9).

We hallow His name because it enshrines His pure and holy character.

As we have seen, the 144,000 do possess the character of Christ.

And in their mouth was found no guile: for they are without fault before the throne of God (Revelation 14:5).

The seal is represented in the forehead because it is a character developed through deep conviction. If the seal of the living God represents God's character reflected in the lives of true believers, then the mark of the beast represents Satan's character in the life. This should come as no surprise, as rather than living a life without sin and possessing no guile, the Bible represents him as the originator of sin (Ezekiel 28:15) and the father of lies (John 8:44).

Manifestly the seal of the living God represents the character of God which will dwell in the hearts of the redeemed at the end of time and the mark of the beast, by contrast, represents the character of Satan which will be planted in the hearts of all those who have not sought the conditions upon which God's grace will be imparted. It is not possible for Christ to take those to heaven at His coming who refuse to permit Him to take sin from their lives. Such would continue to sin in heaven and the entire plan of salvation would thus be thwarted. That plan is to cleanse the universe of sin. This can only be achieved when sin and sinners are no more. God assures us that affliction (sin) will not recur.

> What do ye imagine against the Lord? he will make an utter end: affliction shall not rise up the second time (Nahum 1:9).

We may wonder at the purpose of the question. The answer is clear as we observe the doctrines accepted by most Christians. They imagine that the Lord will not make an end of sin, for they claim that the wicked live on forever in hell. The Bible teaches they will be destroyed (see the book, *The Mystery of Death*, by the same authors).

But what external evidence will indicate the distinction between those who possess the seal of the living God and those cursed with the mark of the beast? The term "seal of the living God" originates from the practice in Bible times of rulers at all levels possessing a distinctive seal of their authority. Each seal contained three mandatory elements:

1. The name of the ruler.

2. The authority of the ruler.

3. The region over which the ruler governed.

When Pilate's seal was placed over the tomb of Christ, it displayed these three mandatory elements: name — Pontius Pilate; authority — governor; region governed — Judea. Similarly, Augustus, the ruler of the Roman Empire, possessed a seal. Its designation stated: name — Caesar Augustus; authority — emperor; region governed — the Roman Empire.

So important is God's seal that He did not commence a word of Scripture before placing His seal upon the words therein.

In the beginning God created the heaven and the earth (Genesis 1:1).

Here all three elements of the Seal of God are incorporated. Name — God; authority — Creator (sometimes referred to as the Maker of all); area governed — the heaven and the earth.

At the conclusion of Creation week the Sabbath was instituted. Here once more the seal of the living God was displayed.

Thus the heavens and the earth were finished, and all the host of them. And on the seventh day God ended his work which he had made: and he rested on the seventh day from all his work which he had made. And God blessed the seventh day and sanctified it: because that in it he had rested from all his work which God created and made (Genesis 2:1-3).

In this passage God's name is inserted three times, His authority is mentioned on four occasions ('make' three times, and 'created' once), and His region of governance once.

Since the ten commandments are a transcript of God's character it comes as no surprise to discover that it contains the seal of the living God. While some commandments contain God's name, the fourth commandment alone contains all three elements.

Remember the Sabbath to keep it holy. Six days shalt thou labour and do all thy work, But the seventh day is the sabbath of Lord thy God: in it thou shalt not do any work, thou, nor thy son, nor thy daughter, thy manservant, nor thy maidservant, nor thy cattle, nor thy stranger that is within thy gates. For in six days the Lord made heaven

and earth, the sea, and all that in them is, and rested the seventh
day: wherefore the Lord blessed the sabbath day, and hallowed it:
(Exodus 20:8-11).

These elements are found in verse 11: God's name — the Lord;
His authority — made; His region of governance — heaven and earth,
the sea and all that in them is.

There is a most important reason why the seal of the living God
is located in the fourth commandment. This commandment commences

Remember the sabbath day to keep it holy (Exodus 20:8).

There is only one manner in which we can truly keep God's
Sabbath and that is in holiness. In order to keep the Sabbath holy,
men must themselves be holy. If one has stolen a hundred dollars
during the week and has not confessed that sin nor made restitution,
no matter how earnestly that individual may worship the Lord on the
holy Sabbath day, he has not kept the Sabbath day holy. It is little
wonder that the Jews referred to Friday as the preparation day. It was
a day to examine each heart and make right any wrongs so that the
Sabbath could be kept in holiness unto the Lord.

Thus the Sabbath is the key to obedience to God's law, for it is
only as we obey each one of the other nine commandments that we
can keep the Sabbath holy. The Sabbath commandment with its in-
trinsic call to a holy life is the only commandment which centers on
our total character. Thus it was most appropriate that God placed His
seal within this commandment, for the seal of the living God is Christ's
character within the heart.

Indeed the entire Bible has as its theme God's loving offer of
the gift of His seal. This is the purpose for its presence in the very
first verse of Scripture. It is the reason that it is found in the very last
message God in His love gives to mankind.

When Christ related the signs of His coming to His disciples,

He made a very important promise which was also a prophecy.

> And this gospel of the kingdom shall be preached in all the world for a witness unto all nations, and then shall the end come (Matthew 24:14).

It will be observed that at this time Christ did not present the precise content of this last message to mankind to be presented prior to His second coming. However, in Revelation this message is expounded. It is termed, for obvious reasons, the three angels' messages. We have already referred to the third angel's message concerning God's wrath upon those who receive the mark of the beast. This is the last of the three angels' messages. The introduction to these messages specifically states that they are the gospel messages to be taken worldwide.

> And I saw another angel fly in the midst of heaven, having the everlasting gospel to preach unto them that dwell on the earth, and to every nation, and kindred, and tongue, and people (Revelation 14:6).

If we examine the first of these angels' messages we discover that it contains the seal of the living God. Indeed the final portion referring to the all-important subject of worship is almost an exact quotation of the last portion of the fourth commandment.

> Saying with a loud voice, Fear God, and give glory to him; for the hour of his judgment is come: and worship him that made heaven, and earth, and the sea, and the fountains of waters (Revelation 14:7).

Notice that this message contains the three mandatory elements of the seal—God's name (God), His authority (made), and the territory of His rulership (heaven and earth, the sea and the fountains of water).

Indeed the great purpose of Scripture is to offer to every human being the seal of the living God, for God is unwilling that any should perish (2 Peter 3:9).

The Sabbath day is of the greatest significance, for full obedience to this commandment ensures a sanctified life.

> Moreover I gave them my sabbaths, to be a sign between me and them, that they might know that I am the Lord that sanctify them (Ezekiel 20:12).

It will be observed in the new earth for only holy people reside there.

> For as the new heavens and the new earth, which I will make, shall remain before me, saith the Lord, so shall your seed and your name remain. And it shall come to pass, that from one new moon to another, and from one sabbath to another, shall all flesh come to worship before me, saith the Lord (Isaiah 66:22, 23).

If Sabbath observance is the external sign of the seal of the living God, then clearly the adherence to a counterfeit Sabbath, one which God has never blessed or hallowed, is the external sign of the mark of the beast at the close of probationary time. Each symbolizes the character of its founder. The seventh-day Sabbath was instituted by Christ; the counterfeit Sabbath promoted in the pope's Apostolic Letter, entered the Christian church via paganism as confirmed by the Baptist author, Edward Hiscox (see Chapter I of this book).

The pope's claim that Sunday worship was instituted to remember the resurrection of Christ carries with it no thread of biblical unction. It is not "Easter which returns week by week," as the pope asserts. If we are to construct a human basis for the selection of a day of worship, some surely would select Friday, the day of Christ's crucifixion. Others would select Thursday, the day of the first Communion service.

It was the lack of Scriptural support for Sunday observance which caused the Council of Trent (convened 1545–1563) to deny the Bible as the lone rule of faith. The Council of Trent was called to counter the Reformation. At one point the bishops present were evenly divided as to whether it would be a good ploy to follow the Protestant lead and declare the Bible as the sole source of faith and doctrine or to retain church authority and tradition, in addition to Scripture, as the rule of faith.

The newly founded Society of Jesus (the Jesuits) perceptively recognized that if the Scriptures alone were the rule of faith, the Catholic Church would lose its mandate for Sunday observance.

The Jesuits found in Cardinal Gaspare de Fosso, Archbishop of Reggio, a city in the "toe" of Italy, one who acknowledged their reasoning. The day following his discussions with the Jesuits, January 18, 1562, Cardinal de Fosso arose in the Council of Trent and stated,

> Such is the condition of the heretics [Protestants] of this age that on nothing do they rely more than that, under the pretence of the Word of God, they overthrow the authority of the Chruch....The authority of the Church, then, is illustrated most clearly by the Scriptures; for while on the one hand she recomends them, declares them to be divine...on the other hand, the legal precepts in the Scriptures taught by the Lord have ceased by virture of the same authority. The Sabbath, the most glorious day of the law, has been changed into the Lord's day.

Here the church authority and church tradition is placed above the Scripture. Cardinal de Fosso's argument swayed the thinking of the assembled bishops and the Council of Trent entrenched church authority as at least equal, and in practice, above Scripture, as its authority for faith, practice, and doctrine.

Unfortunately, the rash of Christian "conversions" from paganism which transpired after the "conversion" of Emperor Constantine, led to the introduction of many pagan religious practices to which a veneer of Christianity was applied. Worship on the first day of the week, Sunday, was just one of these practices. The fact that Christ rose on that day was a convenient veneer to apply to that rite of paganism.

The end-time prophecy of Revelation 13:15-17, warning of the enactment of dire penalties for those who refuse to receive the mark of the beast, is a cause to ponder John Paul's call for civil legislation to ensure Sunday observance. The new canons which call for unspecified penalties for any person who teaches

> ...a doctrine condemned by the Roman Pontiff, or by an ecumenical council, or obstinately rejects the teachings mentioned in Canon 750 s 2, or in Canon 752 and, when warned by the Apostolic See or by the Ordinary, does not retract (Canon 1371 cited in the pope's Apostolic Letter of May 28, 1998 entitled *Ad Tuendam Fidem*),

generate considerable concern for all lovers of the principles of religious liberty and freedom of conscience.

It is time to raise, once more, the cry of religious liberty around the lands of this earth (see the book entitled, *Liberty in the Balance*, authored by Colin and Russell Standish). It is time to study Scripture under the guidance of the Holy Spirit. It is time to make our calling and election sure (2 Peter 1:10). It is time to eschew all non-Scriptural doctrines and practices. It is time to seek God with the whole heart.

We have identified the mark of the beast. We have yet to identify the beast power and the "he" who empowers the beast. The beast will be identified in *Chapter 6 — Identification of the First Beast of Revelation 13.* The "he" will be identified in Chapter 7 of this series — *The Second Beast of Revelation 13.* These are the two superpowers of the end time.

Let us recapitulate the Biblical evidence defining the seal of the living God and mark of the beast.

At the close of earth's history every individual will have heard the everlasting gospel of Revelation 14:6 – 12. It is preached "to every nation, and kindred, and tongue, and people." (Revelation 14:6). Those who accept Christ's salvation receive the seal of the living God. Those who reject it receive the mark of the beast.

Those who receive the seal of the living God will have developed the character of Christ which the Bible summarizes as two characteristics—He did no sin and no guile was found in His mouth (1 Peter 2:22). This is demonstrated in the life by true Sabbathkeeping, for the Sabbath is the commandment of total character, since it may only be kept in holiness. Holiness is the possession of Christ's character.

The mark of the beast is received by those who develop the character of Satan, a character of rebellion against God. This is manifested by observing a counterfeit day of worship—the day of paganism, Sunday, a day of worship for which the Bible provides no mandate.

Those who receive the mark of the beast will be "rewarded" with eternal destruction. This is an act of love by God, for they would never find happiness amongst holy beings, and their continued sin would insure the external pollution of the universe.

Those who receive the seal of the living God receive eternal life; for in Christ's strength and through His spilt blood, they have been fitted for heaven. The choice is ours today.

Chapter 4 — Babylon

Who is the beast? We have noticed the dire mark of the beast in previous chapters in this book. Those who receive the mark of the beast will be subject to the wrath of God. Yet those who refuse to receive the mark of the beast will receive the wrath of the beast. Thus it is most important to identify the beast of Revelation 13.

The Protestant reformers, including Luther, Calvin, Zwingli, Knox, Wesley, and many others, recognized that the beast power was mentioned under various synonyms in Scripture. It was the little horn of Daniel 7, the man of sin, the son of perdition who introduces the mystery of iniquity in 2 Thessalonians 2, the antichrist of 1 John 2 and 4 and 2 John, Babylon of Revelation 14, 16, 17, 18, and the whore and scarlet beast of Revelation 17. (See Part 6.)

The Scripture provides us with so many identifying features of the beast power that there is left to us no possible doubt whatsoever. Remembering the synonymous terms used for the beast as listed above, we find the following identifying factors of the beast.

> After this I saw in the night visions, and behold a fourth beast, dreadful and terrible, and strong exceedingly; and it had great iron teeth: it devoured and brake in pieces, and stamped the residue with the feet

of it: and it was diverse from all the beasts that were before it; and it had ten horns. I considered the horns, and, behold, there came up among them another little horn, before whom there were three of the first horns plucked up by the roots: and, behold, in this horn were eyes like the eyes of man, and a mouth speaking great things (Daniel 7:7,8).

1. Arose from the fourth beast (the Roman Empire) of Daniel 7:7,8.

2. Displaced 3 of the 10 kingdoms into which the Roman Empire disintegrated — Daniel 7:8, 24.

3. Possessed human qualities — Daniel 7:8.

4. Spoke great words — Daniel 7:8.

I beheld, and the same horn made war with the saints, and prevailed against them; Until the Ancient of days came, and judgment was given to the saints of the most High; and the time came that the saints possessed the kingdom. Thus he said, The fourth beast shall be the fourth kingdom upon earth, which shall be diverse from all kingdoms, and shall devour the whole earth, and shall tread it down, and break it in pieces. And the ten horns out of this kingdom are ten kings that shall arise: and another shall rise after them; and he shall be diverse from the first, and he shall subdue three kings. And he shall speak great words against the most High, and shall wear out the saints of the most High, and think to change times and laws: and they shall be given into his hand until a time and times and the dividing of time. But the judgment shall sit, and they shall take away his dominion, to consume and to destroy it unto the end. And the kingdom and dominion, and the greatness of the kingdom under the whole heaven, shall be given to the people of the saints of the most High, whose kingdom is an everlasting kingdom, and all dominions shall serve and obey him. Hitherto is the end of the matter. As for me Daniel, my cogitations much troubled me: but I kept the matter in my heart (Daniel 7:25-28).

5. Made war against God's saints and prevailed against them —

Daniel 7:19-21, 25.

6. That war ceased when the saints possessed the kingdom of God — Daniel 7:22.

7. Is a kingdom — Daniel 7:24.

8. Will be different from the other 10 kingdoms — Daniel 7:24.

9. Shall speak great things against the Most High — Daniel 7:25.

10. Shall change times and laws — Daniel 7:25.

11. Shall possess authority for "time, times, and the dividing of times" — Daniel 7:25.

12. Its dominion shall be taken away in the judgment — Daniel 7:26.

13. It will be utterly destroyed — Daniel 7:26.

Let no man deceive you by any means: for that day shall not come, except there come a falling away first, and that man of sin be revealed, the son of perdition; Who opposeth and exalteth himself above all that is called God, or that is worshipped; so that he as God sitteth in the temple of God, shewing himself that he is God....For the mystery of iniquity doth already work: only he who now letteth will let, until he be taken out of the way. And then shall that Wicked be revealed, whom the Lord shall consume with the spirit of his mouth, and shall destroy with the brightness of his coming: Even him, whose coming is after the working of Satan with all power and signs and lying wonders, And with all deceivableness of unrighteousness in them that perish; because they received not the love of the truth, that they might be saved. And for this cause God shall send them strong delusion, that they should believe a lie (2 Thessalonians 2:3,4,7-11).

14. This power will prevail because of a falling away from the truth — 2 Thessalonians 2:3.

15. Opposes God — 2 Thessalonians 2:4.

16. Exalts itself above God — 2 Thessalonians 2:4.

17. Opposes true worship — 2 Thessalonians 2:4.

18. Sits in the temple of God — 2 Thessalonians 2:4.

19. Accepts the mystery of iniquity — 2 Thessalonians 2:7.

20. Will be destroyed at Christ's coming — 2 Thessalonians 2:8.

21. Will do the works of Satan — 2 Thessalonians 2:9.

22. Will use signs and lying wonders — 2 Thessalonians 2:9.

23. Will do unrighteously — 2 Thessalonians 2: 10.

24. Will accept strong delusions — 2 Thessalonians 2:11.

> Little children, it is the last time: and as ye have heard that antichrist shall come, even now are there many antichrists; whereby we know that it is the last time....Who is a liar but he that denieth that Jesus is the Christ? He is antichrist, that denieth the Father and the Son. Whosoever denieth the Son, the same hath not the Father: But he that acknowledges the Son hath the Father also (1 John 2: 18, 22, 23).

25. Is a liar — 1 John 2:22.

26. Denies the Father and the Son — 1 John 2:22.

> Hereby know ye the Spirit of God: Every spirit that confesseth that Jesus Christ is come in the flesh is of God: And every spirit that confesseth not that Jesus Christ is come in the flesh is not of God: and this is that spirit of antichrist, whereof ye have heard that it should come: and even now already is it in the world (1 John 4:2,3).

27. Denies Christ came in the flesh (fallen nature) — 1 John 4:3,4.

> For many deceivers are entered into the world, who confess not that Jesus Christ is come in the flesh. This is a deceiver and an antichrist (2 John 7).

28. Deceives — 2 John 7.

> And I stood upon the sand of the sea, and saw a beast rise up out of the sea, having seven heads and ten horns, and upon his horns ten crowns, and upon his heads the name of blasphemy. And the beast which I saw was like unto a leopard, and his feet were as the feet of a bear, and his mouth as the mouth of a lion: and the dragon gave him his power, and his seat, and great authority. And I saw one of his heads as it were wounded to death; and his deadly wound was healed: and all the world wondered after the beast. And they worshipped the dragon which gave power unto the beast: and they worshipped the beast, saying, who is like unto the beast? who is able to make war with him? And there was given unto him a mouth speaking great things and blasphemies; and power was given unto him to continue forty and two months. And he opened his mouth in blasphemy against God, to blaspheme his name, and his tabernacle, and them that dwell in heaven. And it was given unto him to make war with the saints, and to overcome them: and power was given him over all kindreds, and tongues, and nations. And all that dwell upon the earth shall worship him, whose names are not written in the book of life of the Lamb slain from the foundation of the world (Revelation 13:1-8).

29. This power rises out of a symbolic sea — Revelation 13:1.

30. Has 7 heads, 10 horns, and 10 crowns — Revelation 13:1.

31. Its name is blasphemy — Revelation 13:1.

32. Has the characteristics of a leopard (Greece — see Daniel 7); a bear (Medo-Persia); and a lion (Babylon) — Revelation 13:2.

33. The dragon (Satan; see Revelation 12:9) gives him power and authority — Revelation 13:2.

34. One of his heads received a deadly wound — Revelation 13:3.

35. The deadly wound was healed — Revelation 13:3.

36. All the world would wonder after the beast — Revelation 13:3.

37. The power leads out in worship of the dragon (Satan; Revelation 12:9; 20:2) — Revelation 13:4.

38. Satan gave him power — Revelation 13:4.

39. The beast itself was worshipped — Revelation 13:4.

40. Other nations were not able to make war with him — Revelation 13:4.

41. He spoke great things and blasphemies — Revelation 13:5.

42. He continues 42 months — Revelation 13:5.

43. Blasphemed the heavenly tabernacle — Revelation 13:6.

44. Blasphemed them that dwell in heaven — Revelation 13:6.

45. Made war with the saints and overcame them — Revelation 13:7.

46. Possessed power over all the world — Revelation 13:7.

47. Will attract almost universal worship — Revelation 13:8.

48. Only the most dedicated of Christians will resist his power and authority — Revelation 13:8.

And I beheld another beast coming up out of the earth; and he had two horns like a lamb, and he spake as a dragon. And he exerciseth all the power of the first beast before him, and causeth the earth and them which dwell therein to worship the first beast, whose deadly wound was healed. And he doeth great wonders, so that he maketh fire come down from heaven on the earth in the sight of men. And deceiveth them that dwell on the earth, by the means of those miracles which he had power to do in the sight of the beast; saying to them that dwell on the earth, that they should make an image to the beast, which had the wound by a sword, and did live. And he had power to give life unto the image of the beast, that the image of the beast should both speak, and cause that as many as would not worship the image of the beast should be killed. And he causeth all, both small and great, rich and poor, free and bond, to receive a mark in their right hand, or in their foreheads: And that no man might buy or sell, save he that had the mark, or the name of the beast, or the number of his name. Here is wisdom. Let him that hath understanding count the number of the beast: for it is the number of a man; and his number is six hundred threescore and six (Revelation 13:11-18).

49. A second power arises exercising all the power of the beast — Revelation 13:11, 12.

50. The beast with the lamb-like horns will force all to worship the first beast — Revelation 13:12.

51. This second beast does great wonders — Revelation 13:13, 14.

52. The second beast deceives — Revelation 13:14.

53. The second beast makes an image to the first beast — Revelation 13:14.

54. The second beast enforces an universal death decree upon all, on behalf of the first beast — Revelation 13:15.

55. The second beast enforces the mark of the first beast — Revelation 13:17.

56. The second beast implements an economic boycott upon all who reject the mark of the beast — Revelation 13:17.

57. The number of the first beast is 666 — Revelation 13:18.

And there followed another angel, saying, Babylon is fallen, is fallen, that great city, because she made all nations drink of the wine of the wrath of her fornication. And the third angel followed them, saying with a loud voice, If any man worship the beast and his image, and receive his mark in his forehead, or in his hand, The same shall drink of the wine of the wrath of God, which is poured out without mixture into the cup of his indignation; and he shall be tormented with fire and brimstone in the presence of the holy angels, and in the presence of the Lamb: And the smoke of their torment ascendeth up for ever and ever: and they have no rest day nor night, who worship the beast and his image, and whosoever receiveth the mark of his name. Here is the patience of the saints: here are they that keep the commandments of God, and the faith of Jesus (Revelation 14:8-12).

58. The beast (Babylon) is fallen because she has made all nations drink of the wine of her fornication — Revelation 14:8.

59. There is fearful retribution for any who receive the mark of the beast — Revelation 14:9-11.

60. The saints who reject the mark of the beast will be those who keep the commandments of God and have Christ's faith — Revelation 14:12.

And I saw as it were a sea of glass mingled with fire: and them that had gotten the victory over the beast, and over his image, and over his mark, and over the number of his name, stand on the sea of glass, having the harps of God. And they sing the song of Moses the servant of God, and the song of the Lamb, saying, Great and marvellous are thy works, Lord God Almighty; just and true are thy ways, thou King of saints (Revelation 15: 2,3).

61. The redeemed will have overcome the beast's mark — Revelation 15:2,3.

And I heard a great voice out of the temple saying to the seven angels, Go your ways, and pour out the vials of the wrath of God upon the earth. And the first went, and poured out his vial upon the earth; and there fell a noisome and grievous sore upon the men which had the mark of the beast, and upon them which worshipped his image....And the great city was divided into three parts, and the cities of the nations fell: and great Babylon came in remembrance before God, to give unto them the cup of the wine of the fierceness of his wrath (Revelation 16:2,3, 19).

62. Those with the mark of the beast receive the seven last plagues — Revelation 16:1,2.

63. It receives the wrath of God — Revelation 16:19.

And there came one of the seven angels which had the seven vials, and talked with me, saying unto me, Come hither; I will shew unto thee the judgment of the great whore that sitteth upon many waters: With whom the kings of the earth have committed fornication, and the inhabitants of the earth have been made drunk with the wine of her fornication. So he carried me away in the spirit into the wilderness: and I saw a woman sit upon a scarlet coloured beast, full of names of blasphemy, having seven heads and ten horns. And the woman was arrayed in purple and scarlet colour, and decked with gold and precious stones and pearls, having a golden cup in her hand full of abominations and filthiness of her fornication: And upon her forehead was a name written, MYSTERY, BABYLON THE GREAT, THE MOTHER OF HARLOTS AND ABOMINATIONS OF THE EARTH. And I saw the woman drunken with the blood of the saints, and with the blood of the martyrs of Jesus: and when I saw her, I wondered with great admiration. And the angel said unto me, Wherefore didst thou marvel? I will tell thee the mystery of the woman, and of the beast that carrieth her, which hath the seven heads and ten horns. The beast that thou sawest was, and is not; and shall ascend out of the bottomless pit, and go into perdition: and they that dwell on the earth shall wonder, whose names were not written in the book of life from the foundation of the world, when they behold the beast that was, and is not, and yet is. And here is the mind which hath wisdom. The seven heads are seven mountains, on which the woman sitteth. And there are seven kings: five are fallen, and one is, and the other is not yet come; and when he cometh, he must continue a short space. And the beast that was, and is not, even he is the eighth, and is of the seven, and goeth into perdition. And the ten horns which thou sawest are ten kings, which have received no kingdom as yet; but receive power as kings one hour with the beast. These have one mind, and shall give their power and strength unto the beast. These shall make war with the Lamb, and the Lamb shall overcome them: for he is Lord of lords, and King of kings: and they that are with him are called, and chosen, and faithful. And he saith unto me, The waters which thou sawest, where the whore sitteth, are peoples, and multitudes, and nations, and tongues. And the ten horns which thou sawest upon the beast, these shall hate the whore, and shall make her desolate and naked, and shall eat her flesh, and burn her with fire. For God hath put in their hearts to fulfil his will, and to agree, and give their kingdom unto the beast, until the words of God shall be fulfilled. And the woman which thou sawest is that great city, which reigneth over the kings of the earth (Revelation 17:1-18).

64. It will be judged — Revelation 17:1.

65. It commits spiritual fornication with national leaders and merchants — Revelation 17:2.

66. It is full of spiritual fornication (see Jeremiah 3:1-6) — Revelation 17:4.

67. The whore is Babylon —Revelation 17:5.

68. It murders saints — Revelation 17:6.

69. It shall be sent to perdition — Revelation 17:8.

70. It sits upon 7 mountains as does the city of Rome — Revelation 17:9.

71. It is one of the seven powers that have opposed God's truth, and returns to associate with the seventh, it being also the eighth — Revelation 17:10,11.

72. These 10 horns, which represent Europe (see Daniel 7:24), shall become united in purpose in order to provide power and authority to the beast — Revelation 17: 12, 13.

73. The 10 horns and the beast make war with God and His people — Revelation 17:14.

74. Eventually the 10 horns will hate the beast and attack it — Revelation 17:15-17.

75. The woman represents a great city which reigns over the world's leaders — Revelation 17:18.

And he cried mightily with a strong voice, saying, Babylon the great is fallen, is fallen, and is become the habitation of devils, and the hold of every foul spirit, and a cage of every unclean and hateful bird. For all nations have drunk of the wine of the wrath of her fornication, and the kings of the earth have committed fornication with her, and the merchants of the earth are waxed rich through the abundance of her delicacies. And I heard another voice from heaven, saying, Come out of her, my people, that ye be not partakers of her sins, and that ye receive not of her plague. For her sins have reached unto heaven, and God hath remembered her iniquities. Reward her even as she rewarded you, and double unto her double according to her works: in the cup which she hath filled fill to her double. How much she hath glorified herself, and lived deliciously, so much torment and sorrow give her: for she saith in her heart, I sit a queen, and am no widow, and shall see no sorrow. Therefore shall her plagues come in one day, death, and mourning, and famine; and she shall be utterly burned with fire: for strong is the Lord God who judgeth her. And the kings of the earth, who have committed fornication and lived deliciously with her, shall bewail her, and lament for her, when they shall see the smoke of her burning, Standing afar off for the fear of her torment, saying, Alas, alas that great city Babylon, that mighty city! for in one hour is thy judgment come. And the merchants of the earth shall weep and mourn over her; for no man buyeth their merchandise any more: The merchandise of gold, and silver, and precious stones, and of pearls, and fine linen, and purple, and silk, and scarlet, and all thyine wood, and all manner vessels of ivory, and all manner vessels of most precious wood, and of brass, and iron, and marble, And cinnamon, odours, and ointments, and frankincense, and wine, oils, and fine flour, and wheat, and beasts, and sheep, and horses, and chariots, and slaves, and souls of men. And the fruits that thy soul lusted after are departed from thee, and all things which were dainty and goodly are departed from thee, and thou shalt find them no more at all. The merchants of these things, which were made rich by her, shall stand afar off for the fear of her torment, weeping and wailing, and saying, Alas, alas that great city, that was clothed in fine linen, and purple, and scarlet, and decked with gold, and precious stones, and pearls! For in one hour so great riches is come to nought. And every shipmaster, and all the company in ships, and sailors, and as many as trade by sea, stood afar off, And cried when they saw the smoke of her burning, saying, What city is like unto this great city! And they cast dust on their heads, and cried, weeping and wailing, saying, Alas, alas that great city, wherein were made rich all that had ships in the sea by reason of her costliness! for in one hour is she made desolate. Rejoice over her, thou heaven, and ye holy apostles and prophets; for God hath avenged you on her. And a mighty angel took up a stone like a great millstone, and cast it into the sea, saying, Thus with violence shall that great city Babylon be thrown down, and shall be found no more at all And the voice of harpers, and musicians, and of pipers, and trumpeters, shall be heard no more at all in thee; and no craftsman, of whatsoever craft he be, shall be found any more in thee; and the sound of a millstone shall be heard no more at all in thee; And the light of a candle shall shine no more at all in thee; and the voice of the bridegroom and of the bride shall be heard no more at all in thee: for thy merchants were the great men of the earth; for by thy sorceries were all nations deceived. And in her was found the blood of prophets, and of saints, and of all that were slain upon the earth (Revelation 18: 2-24).

76. Babylon is vile — Revelation 18:2,3.

77. God urgently calls all men to come out of her faith — Revelation 18:4,5.

78. There will be a terrible retribution for Babylon — Revelation 18:4,5.

79. She has prostituted herself with leaders of nations and merchants and will receive the plagues — Revelation 18:8-24.

And the beast was taken, and with him the false prophet that wrought miracles before him, with which he deceived them that had received the mark of the beast, and them that worshipped his image. These both were cast alive into a lake of fire burning with brimstone (Revelation 19:20).

80. The beast is cast into the lake of fire and brimstone — Revelation 19:20.

And I saw thrones, and they sat upon them, and judgment was given unto them: and I saw the souls of them that were beheaded for the witness of Jesus, and for the word of God, and which had not worshipped the beast, neither his image, neither had received his mark upon their foreheads, or in their hands; and they lived and reigned with Christ a thousand years (Revelation 20:4).

81. Those who reject the work of the beast will reign with God for 1000 years — Revelation 20:4.

The Bible exhibits more than 80 identifying marks of the beast power of Revelation 13. No other symbol is so specifically and irrefutably identified in Scripture. A minority of these identifying features are future, but the great majority are historical facts and thus can be documented. One power, and one only, fulfills all the criteria which have been historically completed — the Roman Catholic Church. The Protestant reformers were absolutely correct in their identification of the beast of Revelation 13 as the antichrist power and their identification of that power as the Papacy.

Martin Luther declared,

We are of the conviction that the Papacy is the seat of the real antichrist (quoted in LeRoy Froom, *The Prophetic Faith of Our Fathers,* Vol.2, p. 256).

John Calvin declared,

I deny him to be the vicar of Christ .... He is antichrist — I deny him to be head of the church (*John Calvin Tracts,* Vol. 1, pp. 219,220).

John Knox stated,

That tyranny which the pope himself has for so many ages exercised over the church, the very antichrist and son of perdition of whom Paul speaks (*The Zurich Letter,* p.199).

John Wesley concluded that

Roman Papacy he [the antichrist] is, in an emphatical sense, the man of sin (John Wesley, *Antichrist and His Ten Kingdoms,* p.110).

These, and other reformers, did not come to this conclusion because of a desire to vilify the Roman Catholic Church. They were not simply taking a cheap shot at that church. Their writings reveal that they had carefully studied the evidence of Scripture and were forced by weight of that evidence to conclude that only the Roman Catholic Church fitted the criteria. Protestants of the present day who still recognize this fact are frequently accused of paranoia, papalphobia, by fellow Protestants who have taken no pains to study Scripture in relation to the matter and are caught up in the evil spirit of ecumenism.

The majority of Protestants who intelligently identify the beast of Revelation 13 as the Papacy have a deep love for the souls of their Roman Catholic friends. They recognize that many Roman Catholics are sincere in their convictions, but deceived. Recognizing Christ's plaintive plea,

> Come out of her *my* people, that ye be not partakers of her sins, and that ye receive not of her plagues (Revelation 18:4, emphasis added),

we must clearly make the identification. It is painful to so identify such a popular religion, but no true Christian can refrain from presenting such an urgent, loving call, from God. It is no display of love for Roman Catholics to conceal that which Scripture reveals.

The Roman Catholic Church is the result of the paganization of Christianity which progressed rapidly from the fourth century. The focal point of the entry of paganism into the Christian Church was the "conversion" of the Roman Emperor Constantine in 321 A.D. Hordes of European pagans entered the fold, encouraged by the conversion of their emperor. But in most cases there was no heart conversion, no new birth experience. They desired to continue to practice their pagan worship within Christianity. Thus they introduced their day of worship, Sunday, sanitizing it as a memorial of Christ's resurrection. They introduced their idol worship, covering its pagan nature by providing Christian names for the idols, such as Mary, the apostles and Christ Himself. They introduced the pagan practice of sprinkling water on the head of the newborn in order to remove evil from them and designated this pagan practice, Christian baptism. Also, the relating of one's sins to the priests entered the Christian faith. The Bible concept of Christ as our only Mediator was lost.

> For there is one God, and one mediator between God and men, the man Christ Jesus (1 Timothy 2:5).

The idea that the soul is immortal, borrowed from paganism, and defying the plain word of Scripture, was introduced. God alone has immortality.

> Which in his times he shall shew, who is the blessed and only Potentate, the King of kings, and Lord of lords; Who only hath immortality, dwelling in the light which no man can approach unto; whom no man hath seen, nor can see: to whom be honour and power everlasting. Amen (1 Timothy 6: 15,16),

This led to the belief that virtuous men and women go to heaven when they die and the evil go to ever-burning torment. Christ plainly taught that we are united with Him, if faithful, not at death, but when He comes again.

> Let not your heart be troubled: ye believe in God, believe also in me. In my Father's house are many mansions: if it were not so, I would have told you. I go to prepare a place for you. And if I go and prepare a place for you, I will come again, and receive you unto myself; that where I am, there ye may be also (John 14:1-3).

He also states clearly that the punishment of the wicked is eternal destruction.

> Who shall be punished with everlasting destruction from the presence of the Lord, and from the glory of his power (2 Thessalonians 1:9).

The Bible knows nothing of the pagan concept of purgatory. Neither does the Bible provide salvation on the basis of monetary gifts.

> For by grace are ye saved through faith; and that not of yourselves: it is the gift of God; Not of works, lest any man should boast. For we are his workmanship, created in Christ Jesus unto good works, which God hath before ordained that we should walk in them. (Ephesians 2:8-10).

> But we are bound to give thanks alway to God for you, brethren beloved of the Lord, because God hath from the beginning chosen you to salvation through sanctification of the Spirit and belief of the truth (2 Thessalonians 2:13).

Nor does Scripture give the right to any human to destroy God's law. Any Roman Catholic can examine the Ten Commandments in a Catholic version of Scripture, such as the Douay or the Jerusalem Bibles, and read the true Ten Commandments. But in their catechisms they are taught to entirely discard the second commandment, to eliminate most of the fourth commandment and to divide the tenth commandment in two in order to preserve the number of ten commandments. The reason that the pope's Apostolic Letter, *Dies Domini*, repeatedly refers to the Sabbath commandment as the third commandment rather than the fourth is because Catholicism has cast out the second commandment which states

> Thou shalt not make unto thee any graven image, or any likeness of any thing that is in heaven above, or that is in the earth beneath, or that is in the water under the earth: Thou shalt not bow down thyself to them, nor serve them: for I the Lord the God am a jealous God, visiting the iniquity of the fathers upon the children unto the third and fourth generation of them that hate me; And shewing mercy unto thousands of them that love me, and keep my commandments (Exodus 20:4-6).

There is sound evidence to charge the Roman Catholic Church with the introduction of idolatry into the faith. Some claim that their veneration of idols is not evidence of idol worship. If this claim is valid, why then did the Roman Catholic Church think it necessary to expunge the second commandment from the Decalogue?

Further, the Roman Catholic Church has altered the Sabbath commandment in their catechisms with the words, "Remember the sabbath day to keep it holy." The full fourth commandment is,

> Remember the sabbath day to keep it holy. Six days shalt thou labour, and do all thy work: But the seventh day is the sabbath of the Lord thy God: in it thou shalt not do any work, thou, nor thy son, nor thy daughter, thy manservant, nor thy maidservant, nor thy cattle, nor thy stranger that is within thy gates: For in six days the Lord made heaven and earth, the sea, and all that in them is, and rested the seventh day: wherefore the Lord blessed the sabbath day, and hallowed it (Exodus 20: 8-11).

Here again is compelling evidence that the Roman Catholic Church full well knows that Sunday worship does not extend back to apostolic times, otherwise it would have been the apostles who would have initiated such an alteration. The apostles spoke often of keeping the commandments, but made no effort to alter them. A few examples include the words of Paul.

> Circumcision is nothing, and uncircumcision is nothing, but the keeping of the commandments of God (1 Corinthians 7:19),

John stated,

> And hereby we do know that we know him, if we keep his commandments. He that saith, I know him, and keep not his commandments, is a liar, and the truth is not in him. (1 John 2:3,4).

> And he that keepeth his commandments dwelleth in him, and he in him. And hereby we know that he abideth in us, by the Spirit which he hath given us (1 John 3:24).

> By this we know that we love the children of God, when we love God and keep his commandments. For this is the love of God, that we keep his commandments: and his commandments are not grievous (1 John 5:2,3)

> And this is love, that we walk after his commandments. This is the

commandment, That, as ye have heard from the beginning, ye should walk in it (2 John 6).

And the dragon was wroth with the woman, and went to make war with the remnant of her seed, which keep the commandments of God, and have the testimony of Jesus Christ (Revelation 12:17)

Here is the patience of the saints: here are they that keep the commandments of God, and the faith of Jesus (Revelation 14:12).

Blessed are they that do his commandments, that they may have right to the tree of life, and may enter in through the gates into the city (Revelation 22:14).

Combining the concepts of the immortality of the soul, christening to remove original sin and eternal punishment in hell, the early Roman Catholic Church taught that all innocent but unbaptized children who died were doomed to eternal torment. Later, the concept was softened by consigning such unfortunate children to a mythical entity called limbo, simply because of the neglect of their parents to have their heads sprinkled with water. It is little wonder that the French fled from such an arbitrary and vengeful "god" and rather embraced the prostituted goddess of mercy at the time of the French Revolution.

It must not be forgotten that one of the identifying features of the little horn of Daniel 7 is that this power would "think to change times and laws" (Daniel 7:15). Certainly the Papacy has emphatically fulfilled that criterion without the least question, as it has eliminated the second commandment from God's sacred law removed much of the fourth commandment which deals with God, holy times, and divided the tenth commandment.

We will see that in other ways the Papacy, and the Papacy alone, fulfills the 81 criteria of the beast power of Revelation 13.

Chapter 5 — The Wine of Babylon's Fornication

And there followed another angel, saying, Babylon is fallen, is fallen, that great city, because she made all nations drink of the wine of the wrath of her fornication (Revelation 14:8).

This is to many, one of the most puzzling texts of Scripture. It is remarkable that a message concerning Babylon should be proclaimed in God's last and greatest message of love to the world. After all Babylon was utterly destroyed, never to rise again, 2,500 years ago. The fall of Babylon is hardly the latest news. And then we are confounded by the wine of the wrath of Babylon's fornication. What could that possibly be?

Many earnest Bible students give up in despair and move to other areas of Scripture. But we need not react in such a fashion. The Bible is its own interpreter and thus divine understanding may be sought.

The serious searcher for truth is provided with two substantial clues to the unraveling of this apparently incomprehensible verse of Scripture. It is these clues which lead us to a clear and positive understanding of this verse. We discover a number of prophecies which foretold the fall of the literal Babylonian Empire 2,500 years ago. Two of these attract our attention. The first, "Babylon is fallen, is fallen" (Isaiah 20:9), contains precisely the same words as found in the second angel's message which prophecies the destruction of spiritual Babylon.

Further, the wine of Babylon's fornication was also found in literal Babylon.

> Babylon hath been a golden cup in the Lord's hand, that made all the earth drunken: the nations have drunken of her wine; therefore the nations are mad (Jeremiah 51:7).

Also notice the following verse,

> Babylon is suddenly fallen and destroyed (Jeremiah 51:8).

Since the cardinal elements of the second angel's message are found in prophecies relating to the fall of literal Babylon, wisdom dictates that we direct our attention to that fall in order to unravel the apparent mystery of the second angel's message. In this search we are fortunate to discover that God has provided an entire chapter of the Bible in which the last few hours of the kingdom of Babylon are described.

Let us examine the train of events in place just a few hours before Darius, leading the Medo-Persian armies, destroyed Babylon.

> Belshazzar the king made a great feast to a thousand of his lords, and drank wine before the thousand (Daniel 5:1).

The king and his lords were attending a great feast. Indeed it was a drunken orgy. It will be observed that the focus of that feast was *wine* — the wine of the wrath of Babylon's fornication!

Notice,

> Belshazzar, whiles he tasted the wine, commanded to bring the golden and silver vessels which his father Nebuchadnezzar had taken out of the temple which was in Jerusalem; that the king, and his princes,

his wives, and his concubines, might drink therein. Then they brought the golden vessels that were taken out of the temple of the house of God which was at Jerusalem; and the king, and his princes, his wives, and his concubines, drank in them. They drank wine, and praised the gods of gold, and of silver, of brass, of iron, of wood, and of stone (Daniel 5:2 – 4).

Here is carefully described the wine of the wrath of Babylon's fornication. This blasphemous King Belshazzar, not content to besottle his mind with wine alone, deigned to bring the sacred vessels plundered from the temple of God and use them as receptacles for the wine. These vessels had been solemnly dedicated to a high and holy function. Some were receptacles for the blood of the sacrifice which represented the pure and sinless life of our Lord and Saviour, Jesus Christ. Other vessels held the drink offerings of unfermented wine — the pure juice of the grape which also represented Christ's pure spilt blood offered for our sins on Calvary. No alcohol was permitted in these offerings, for fermentation was a symbol of sin. Such an offering would have defiled the sacred services of the temple.

But this profligate king had placed the symbol of sin, alcoholic wine, within the sacred vessels, in which such wine had no place whatsoever. Those today who utilize alcoholic wine in the communion service should reflect that they are following the example of that Babylonian potentate. God could not longer permit such open defiance and the purposeful desecration of the sacred symbolism of Christ's redeeming sacrifice.

In placing in the sacred vessels the symbol of sin (alcoholic wine — the wine of the wrath of Babylon's fornication), King Belshazzar had united truth with error, the religion of God with the paganism of Satan, the sacred with the profane. Belshazzar had doomed his kingdom. Furthermore, in offering this unholy admixture of truth and error as worship to the Babylonian idols, the king defined the religion of Babylon — the wine of the wrath of her fornication.

While the empire and city of Babylon were destroyed in 539 B.C., its religious principles have pervaded the world ever since, first in Euro-Asian paganism and later, by infiltration, into Christianity. Even many Protestants, today, follow many of the non-Scriptural pagan practices such as Sunday worship, infant baptism, a belief in the immortality of the soul and that at death one either is awarded everlasting life or everlasting torment, as well as the concept of original sin together with other pagan beliefs which now pervade the Christian faith. What a warning God's announcement that Babylon is fallen is to each of us! In these last days of earth's history our God is calling us to forsake any religion which unites God's faith with paganism, truth with error, and the sacred with the profane. His call is clearly stated.

> Wherefore, beloved, seeing that ye look for such things, be diligent that ye may be found of him in peace, without spot, and blameless (2 Peter 3:14).

> Husbands, love your wives, even as Christ also loved the church, and gave himself for it; That he might sanctify and cleanse it with the washing of water by the word. That he might present it to himself a glorious church, not having spot, or wrinkle, or any such thing; but that it should be holy and without blemish. (Ephesians 5:25-27).

Today men may rationalize their effort to worship God in a religion which couples Christ's truth with Satanic paganism; they may even rejoice in it. But the second angel's message is the handwriting on the wall for those who initiate the religion of Babylon. When that handwriting is seen and clearly understood there will be no rejoicing nor charismatic revelry. As Belshazzar was aroused from his drunkenness, so too will we be aroused from our spiritual blindness.

> In the same hour came forth fingers of a man's hand, and wrote over against the candlestick upon the plaster of the wall of the king's palace: and the king saw the part of the hand that wrote. Then the king's countenance was changed, and his thoughts troubled him, so that

the joints of his loins were loosed, and his knees smote one against another (Daniel 5: 5,6).

The prophet Daniel plainly declared the meaning of the hand-writing which was upon the wall.

And this is the writing that was written, MENE, MENE, TEKEL, UPHARSIN. This is the interpretation of the thing: MENE; God hath numbered thy kingdom, and finished it. TEKEL; Thou art weighed in the balances, and art found wanting. PERES; Thy kingdom is divided, and given to the Medes and Persians (Daniel 5:25-28).

Weighed in the balances and found wanting? Why did God use such terminology? God has called for a pure people, men and women who will serve Him with the whole heart. For the unconverted mind such a standard was unpalatable. These individuals still desired heaven. They wished the assurance of salvation without the need to prepare to live with the high and holy beings of heaven. They found men who examined the desires of their own unconverted hearts rather than God, who set themselves up as possessors of spiritual knowledge, who provided men and women with the assurance they desired.

The people had descended from Noah. The events of the world-wide Flood were a testimony to the fact that God would not forever tolerate sin in the lives of infidels and professing followers of God. Yet, once more, they followed the perilous course of uniting sin with righteousness, salving their consciences with the belief that a loving God would accept them in their sin so long as they professed to follow Him.

In Babylon the concept was accepted that one did not need to live a pure and holy life in the power of God. The priests of Babylon asserted that men and women could achieve salvation so long as there was more good in their lives than evil. This calmed the consciences of some, but not all. As men reached old age or felt they were suffering a terminal illness, the touted assurance of the Babylonian theory of salvation often dissipated, for these individuals possessed no way of measuring their good deeds or their evil deeds.

In despair, they sought the judgment of the Babylonian priests. Naturally, the priests requested them to relate their major good deeds and their salient evil deeds, and then made a human judgment of whether these poor individuals had performed more good or bad deeds in their lives. This process became known as weighing in the balances. If the priest evaluated that the individual was weighing heavily on the side of good, then salvation was assured. If it was judged that he was weighing heavily on the side of evil, then he was doomed to eternal damnation.

Not surprisingly, the latter individuals beseeched the priests in order to learn how they could redress the balance. Logically the priest stated that a "heavy" good deed or deeds were required before the hypothetical balance would weigh heavily on the side of good and salvation be assured. The priests were not lost for suggestions. If a temple was under construction, a sizeable donation to assist in this project was suggested as possessing the required weight to redress the balance. Soon the wily Babylonian priests recognized the economic value in weighing all the good deeds lightly and the evil deeds heavily.

Thus paganism commenced the practice of the confession of one's sin to a priest and the so called sacrament of penance, two further pagan concepts which have entered the Christian church from paganism. God, recognizing the nature of King Belshazzar's religion, used terminology which he would pointedly understand — "Thou art weighed in the balances and found wanting." For him there remained no great good deed by which he could reverse the balance. He was lost and lost eternally. Scripture records no last-minute confession and no return to the religion of Jehovah which his grandfather, King Nebuchadnezzar, had accepted at the end of his life and which Belshazzar well knew. After relating God's grace extended to

Nebuchnezzar, Daniel sternly told his grandson (spoken of here in the ancestral sense as his son, just as Christ was called the son of David),

> And thou his son, O Belshazzar, hast not humbled thine heart, though thou knewest all this (Daniel 5:22).

Thus the second angel's message calls men and women who love the Lord to depart from a faith which unites Christianity with paganism. Indeed He is now pleading for all to come out of such faiths.

> And after these things I saw another angel come down from heaven, having great power; and the earth was lightened with his glory. And he cried mightily with a strong voice, saying, Babylon the great is fallen, is fallen, and is become the habitation of devils, and the hold of every foul spirit, and a cage of every unclean and hateful bird. For all nations have drunk of the wine of the wrath of her fornication, and the kings of the earth have committed fornication with her, and the merchants of the earth are waxed rich through the abundance of her delicacies. And I heard another voice from heaven, saying, Come out of her, my people, that ye be not partakers of her sins, and that ye receive not of her plagues. For her sins have reached unto heaven, and God hath remembered her iniquities (Revelation 18:1-5).

These are impelling words.

Earlier we demonstrated that the first angel's message was a call to accept the seal of the living God, for it contains His name ("God"), His authority ("made" — the Creator), and His dominion ("heaven, and earth, and the sea, and the fountains of waters"). The third angel's message is a plea to reject Satan's seal — the mark of the beast. The centrality of the second angel's message is, indeed, properly placed. Our eternal destinies will rest upon the issue of our relationship to the religion of Babylon. If we accept that religion we will receive Satan's seal, the mark of the beast, his character in our lives externally evidenced by breaking the seventh-day Sabbath commandment and accepting the counterfeit Sabbath of Sunday.

Those who reject the religion of Babylon will permit the Holy Spirit to mold their characters so that they possess the character of Jesus. They will thus receive the seal of the living God which is evidenced externally by holy Sabbath observance. It is little wonder that the three angels' messages, God's last call to mankind, are concluded by the words,

Here is the patience of the saints: here are they that keep the commandments of God, and the faith of Jesus (Revelation 14:12).

Today God's call is for us to seek His seal, to yield to Him so that by His grace, salvation may be ours. His plea is for us to desist from all improper practices and eschew pagan doctrinal concepts and to worship Him in spirit and in truth (John 4:23). Such will not yield to the Pope's call for Sunday observance and will resist Sunday enforcement.

Chapter 6 — Identification of the First Beast of Revelation 13

W e have already asserted that the 81 criteria of identification of the beast of Revelation 13 all point to the Church of Rome. But it is essential that this fact be verified. Lest there be a question that the little horn, the man of sin and son of perdition, the antichrist, the beast of Revelation 13, Babylon, the beast of Revelation 17, and the woman 'riding on the beast' are synonymous terms, a table of their common criteria which will appear at the conclusion of this chapter should put any queries to rest.

It would be tedious to trace all 81 criteria in a brief account such as this, and it is not necessary. Some of the 81 criteria, if taken in isolation could apply to other entities beside the Papacy. For example, the criterion,

> And it was given unto him to make war with the saints, and to overcome them" (Revelation 13:7)

certainly is applicable to the Roman Catholic Church. Estimates of those destroyed by its vengeance range from 50 - 120 million. But it could justifiably be applied to communism, to Emperor Nero, Emperor Diocletian, or others as well.

Let us, therefore, examine just those criteria which can be applied to the Roman Catholic Church and it alone. We will notice Daniel's precise description of the little horn power.

> Then I would know the truth of the fourth beast, which was diverse from all the others, exceeding dreadful, whose teeth were of iron, and his nails of brass; which devoured, brake in pieces, and stamped the residue with his feet; And of the ten horns that were in his head, and of the other which came up, and before whom three fell; even of that horn that had eyes, and a mouth that spake very great things, whose look was more stout than his fellows.... And the ten horns out of this kingdom are ten kings that shall arise: and another shall rise after them; and he shall be diverse from the first, and he shall subdue three kings. And he shall speak great words against the most High, and shall wear out the saints of the most High, and think to change times and laws: and they shall be given into his hand until a time and times and the dividing of time (Daniel 7: 19,20,24,25).

A number of criteria are presented in these verses. We will highlight three of these. The first is that the little horn arose out of the 10 horns of the fourth beast, representative of Imperial Rome. These 10 horns are the 10 kings (kingdoms) which arose in Europe as the Roman Empire disintegrated (Daniel 7:24). The second criterion is that the little horn would uproot three of the other horns so that it could emerge (Daniel 7: 20,24). The third criterion upon which we wish to focus is that this power would continue for the mysterious period of "a time, times and the dividing of time" (Daniel 7:25).

The first criterion is disposed of easily. History attests that ten nations of Western Europe replaced the Roman Empire upon its fall. These nations, with their modern-day descendants in parentheses, were the Alemmani (Germans), Anglo-Saxons (English), Burgundians (Swiss), Franks (French), Heruli, Lombards (Italians), Ostrogoths, Suevi (Portuguese), Vandals, and Visigoths (Spanish).

Now let us examine the third criterion, the apparently imprecise and nonspecific period of the little horn's era of dominance. We are plainly told that the little horn has dominion for a time, times, and the dividing of time. The *Complete Oxford Dictionary* defines the term "time" as used in Daniel 7 as "a space of time generally understood to be a year."

Accepting the Oxford Dictionary's definition, which later we will determine is consistent with Scripture, then a time equals one year. Clearly times means a number of years, but how many? Two? Three? Five? Ten? The dividing of time refers to a fraction of a year. Again we have insufficient evidence to determine that fraction. Providentially, the same period is cited seven times in Scripture. We can promptly solve the fraction of a year delineated as the "dividing of time" for two of the remaining passages refer to this period in similar terminology designating it as "time, times, and an half" (Daniel 12:7), and "a time, and times, and half a time" (Revelation 12:14).

Manifestly the fraction of a year is one half. We can also discern "the meaning of times" by reference to two parallel terms for the same period. This term for the total period is "forty and two months" (Revelation 11:2; 13:5). It should come as no surprise to learn that the same period in describing the little horn power of Daniel 7 is also specified in Revelation 13 in describing the beast power, for they are synonymous symbols.

Now by a matter of simple mathematics we are able to learn that the "times" of Daniel 7 represents two years, for the "time" represents 12 months and the "dividing of time" equals six months. Thus the remaining period of "times" must amount to 24 months in order that the total equal 42 months.

But we are faced with yet another question. How many days are there in each of these 42 months? The Jews used equal months of 30 days with 360 days per year. Is this a Jewish year, or a solar year which contains 365 days, 5 hours, 48 minutes and 46 seconds? Another question is whether we can be certain that there were 30 days in a Jewish month. Does Scripture so testify? Yes, it does. Referring to the flood in the time of Noah we are told,

In the six hundredth year of Noah's life, in the second month, the seventeenth day of the month, the same day were all the fountains of the great deep broken up, and the windows of heaven were opened (Genesis 7:11).

Thus the flood commenced on the 17th day of the second month. The waters abated precisely five months later.

And the ark rested in the seventh month, on the seventeenth day of the month, upon the mountains of Ararat (Genesis 8:4).

How many days were involved in this five-month period? Helpfully, God provides us with the answer.

And the waters returned from off the earth continually: and after the end of the hundred and fifty days the waters were abated (Genesis 8:3).

Thus the five-month period consisted of exactly 150 days — 30 days per month.

To further confirm this fact, the period mentioned in Daniel 7 is found in two other passages of Scripture in addition to the five already quoted. Both of these refer to the period as

...a thousand two hundred and three score days (Revelation 11:3; 12:6).

Since a score is 20, the period specified is 1260 days. This concurs with the fact that 42 months of 30 days equals 1,260 days.

The Bible is a magnificent book. It surely is its own interpreter. What appeared to be a baffling time period of "a time and times and the dividing of time" has been elucidated by the Word of God itself. It is a period of 1,260 days. The Bible also assists us in discovering the interpretation of this period of Daniel's prophecy. The prophet Ezekiel was a contemporary of Daniel. Indeed, Ezekiel refers to Daniel three times in his prophecy (Ezekiel 14:14,20; 28:3). In his prophetic book he states that

I [God] have appointed thee a day for a year (Ezekiel 4:6).

Furthermore, the application of that principle in the time prophecies of Daniel has proven to be accurate.

Thus the Scripture prophesied that the little horn/beast power would be dominant for 1,260 years. There have been many mighty empires upon earth. The Roman Empire was dominant for about 500 years, the British Empire for two or three hundred years and other empires for lesser times. Only, apart from the Papacy, does the Holy Roman Empire approach this duration of time. It commenced with the coronation of Charlemagne in 800 by Pope Leo III and was dissolved when Emperor Francis II abdicated in 1806 — a period of 1,006 years, 254 years short of the 1,260 year period.

Before we move on to verify the fact that the Papacy did dominate Europe for precisely 1,260 years and that three of the ten nations which arose out of the decline of the Roman Empire were uprooted, let us examine the tremendous Biblical scholarship of two of the early church fathers in the conclusions they drew concerning the rise of antichrist. We do not, of course, base the exposition of Scripture upon the writings of humans, but, nevertheless, the insights of these two men were outstanding.

Tertullian (155 -222) wrote of the Roman Empire "whose separation into ten kingdoms will bring on antichrist. This is an outstanding understanding. During the life of Tertullian the Roman Empire was powerful, and its demise could not have been predicted. But, clearly, Tertullian was a man of Scripture and he believed God's word. Further, he had correctly linked the little horn of Daniel 7 with the antichrist of 1 John 2 and 4, and 2 John.

Cyril of Jerusalem (315-386) stated,

There shall arise, at the same time, ten kingdoms of the Romans at different places indeed, the reigning all of them at the same time. After them the eleventh will be antichrist, who through magical wickedness, will seize the power of the Romans.

Cyril also united Daniel 7 with 1 John and 2 John. Like Tertullian he recognized the fourth beast of Daniel 7 as the Roman Empire, following the first three beasts which symbolized Babylon, Medo-Persia, and Greece, respectively.

The fall of the Roman Empire is dated at 476 A.D. The Emperor was situated in Constantinople. In 533, Emperor Justinian, rather inconsequentially at the time, declared the Bishop of Rome to be "the first rank of all bishops." But Pope John II (533-535) was totally paralyzed by the conquest of Rome by the Ostrogoths. There was no manner in which he could exercise this vested preeminence, which had settled the long running rivalry for that honor between the Bishops of Rome and Constantinople. His successor, Agapetus I (535-536), in his brief stay in the post was equally prevented from seizing the authority granted. So too was Pope Silvanus (536-537). But in 538 A.D., the recently crowned Pope Virgilius (537-555) seized the power with the defeat and expulsion of the Ostrogoths from Rome. Papal politico-religious authority was now fully established for the first time. Thus the year 538 A.D. marks the commencement of Papal dominance in Europe.

It is significant that Pope Virgilius was the first pope who was not canonized. This no doubt was due for the secular nature of his past, for the popes had earlier been invested with the title Pontifex Maximus — the Supreme Pontiff.

But which three nations were uprooted by the rise of the papal power? Earlier we listed the ten kingdoms which supplanted the Roman Empire and noted the races represented in modern Western Europe. But three of those nations have no representation today in Europe. Incredibly, one of those is the Ostrogoths who were sufficiently powerful up to 538 A.D. that they occupied Rome. Yet God's word is absolutely certain. Did the Heruli, Ostrogoths, and Vandals vanish in the wake of the rise of papal power in Europe in the sixth century A.D.? We quote the *Encyclopedia Brittanica,* 1990 edition. Under the subject 'Heruli' this authority states, "The mid-sixth century they vanished from history." Of the Ostrogoths the same source states that they were "extinct before 554." Finally the *Encyclopedia Brittanica* records the fact that the Vandals "maintained a kingdom...from 429-524."

History attests to the certain fulfillment of prophecy. Did the Papacy continue to assert power for 1,260 years? Indeed it did. Napoleon Bonaparte was determined to demolish the Papacy.

In 1797 Napoleon Bonaparte imposed the Treaty of Tolentino on the Pope....In the next year [1798] General Berthier, Napoleon's chief of staff, seized Rome and established the Roman Republic. On the grounds that the Pope's preserve in Rome might provoke a counter-revolution, the French ordered Pius VI to leave the Vatican. He was escorted to Sienna, and then across the Alps to France. (*Collins Encyclopedia* 1990, subject 'Papacy').

Pope Pius was desperately ill in 1797. His physicians expected his death that year, but he recovered. Napoleon was awaiting his death in order to abolish the Papacy. Had the Pope died that year the prophecy would have been inaccurate by one year. God does not deal in approximations. Pius VI died in captivity in 1799. Understanding the matter, Joseph Rickeby, *The Modern Papacy*, Vol. 3, Lecture 24, p. 1, stated,

Half Europe thought Napoleon's veto would be obeyed and that with the Pope the Papacy was dead.

Scripture describes this demolition of the Papacy as "the deadly wound." But while men believed the Papacy had received a fatal blow, our all-seeing God knew otherwise.

And I stood upon the sand of the sea, and saw a beast rise up out of the sea, having seven heads and ten horns, and upon his horns ten crowns, and upon his heads the name of blasphemy. And the beast which I saw was like unto a leopard, and his feet were as the feet of a bear, and his mouth as the mouth of a lion: and the dragon gave him his power, and his seat, and great authority. And I saw one of his heads as it were wounded to death; and his deadly wound was healed: and all the world wondered after the beast (Revelation 13:1-3).

Notice that this beast inculcated into its system all the evil of Greece (the leopard beast of Daniel 7:6), Medo-Persia (the bear beast of Daniel 7:5), and Babylon (the lion beast of Daniel 7:4), all of which defied the God of heaven. But God foresaw that the apparent deadly wound would be healed. For precisely 1260 years (538-1798) the beast power had ruled supreme. It was not yet to be totally destroyed.

Indeed the healing process was commenced only two years after the Pope's arrest and one year after his death. Military reverses caused Napoleon to recall the battalion of troops in Rome under the command of his brother, Joseph Bonaparte, in 1800. Shortly after, the cardinals returned and elected Pope Pius VII. The Papacy was weak and impotent but a thread of life was restored. Incredibly, Napoleon invited the Pope to crown him Emperor. Impulsively at the last moment, Napoleon grasped the crown out of the Pope's hands and crowned himself, but he did bestow upon the Pope the two massive and magnificent porcelain candlesticks, eight feet in height, which had lighted his throne during the coronation ceremony in Notre Dame Cathedral. This gift is still on display in the Vatican Museum.

The road to restoration of the Papacy was a rocky one. In 1870, Garibaldi, in uniting the various states of Italy, wrested the papal states from Vatican control. The Papacy had lost its last vestige of temporal sovereignty. But in 1929, sovereignty was restored by Benito Mussolini, the Prime Minister of Italy, when he signed the Concordat with the Vatican Secretary of State, Cardinal de Gaspari, according political independence to this territory formally within Italy, an area of 108 acres (just over 40 hectares). The San Franciso Chronicle announced the event with the following headline:

Heal Wound of Many Years—Vatican At Peace With Italy After Many Years.

While the Vatican is the smallest nation upon earth, it has diplomatic relations with more nations than any other country. Its influence and popularity has risen to the point where one cannot even discern the scar of the deadly wound. In truth all the world *is* wondering after the beast in a manner never before attained by the Papacy. Buddhists, Hindus, Jews, Moslems and of course, Protestants, are tracking to the Vatican in honor of the Pope and his papal system. His visits to non-Christian nations such as India, Singapore and Thailand have drawn record crowds as citizens struggled to catch a glimpse of him. His power is so great that *Time* magazine (February 24, 1992) credited him with bringing down Communism through his vast intelligence system of prelates, priests, and faithful laity. This system is in place in the great majority of nations upon earth.

But does the Vatican have designs upon world leadership? Indeed it does! In his classic work, *The Keys of This Blood* (Touchstone, New York, 1991), Dr. Malachi Martin outlines the inner aims of the Papacy. Dr. Martin is no minor figure. He is a Roman Catholic priest who has served in the Vatican and has an intimate knowledge of its inner workings. He is highly regarded in his own church. His book lists his background as follows:

Malachi Martin, eminent theologian, expert on the Catholic Church. Former Jesuit and professor at the Vatican's Pontifical Biblical Institute, is the author of the national best-sellers *Vatican, The Final Conclave, Hostage to the Devil* and *The Jesuits.* He was trained in theology at Louvain. There he received his doctorates in Semitic Languages, Archaeology, and Oriental History. He subsequently studied at Oxford and Hebrew University in Jerusalem. From 1958 to 1964 he served in Rome, where he was a close associate of the renowned Jesuit cardinal Augustin Bea and Pope John XXIII. He now lives in New York City. (Malachi Martin, op. cit.)

His book commences with the startling words,

Willing or not, ready or not, we are all involved in an all-out, no-holds-barred, three-way global competition. Most of us are not competitors, however. We are the stakes. For the competition is about who will establish the first one-world system of government that has ever existed in the society of nations. It is about who will hold and wield the dual power of authority and control over each of us as individuals and over all of us together as a community; over the entire six billion people expected by demographers to inhabit the earth by early in the third millennium. (Ibid. p. 15)

Dr. Martin makes it clear that the three competitors for world supremacy are the Vatican, Western Capitalism led by the United States, and Communism. He leaves no doubt that he is convinced that the Vatican will emerge the victor. In this view he is supported, as we have seen, by Scripture. Had Dr. Martin written his book a couple of years later, undoubtedly he would have declared that Communism no longer posed a serious threat to the other two "competitors." But we shall see that Scripture reveals that the Vatican and the United States, rather than being competitors are embracing the role of colaborers in this move towards global dominance. And make no mistake, this global dominance will be of a most compulsive nature. As Dr. Martin states,

The competition is all-out because, now that it has started, there is no way it can be reversed or called off. No holds are barred because, once the competition has been decided, the world and all that's in it—our way of life as individuals and as citizens of the nations; our educational systems and our religions and our cultures; even the badges of our national identity, which most of us have always taken for granted—all will have been powerfully and radically altered forever. No one can be exempted from its effects. No sector of our lives will remain untouched. (Ibid., p.15)

This is globalism at its zenith. It embodies aims for a global government, global economy, global educational system, a global religion, and a global culture. In order to enforce each of these aims, a global legal system would be required.

One glance at the European Union which Lars Bergquist, Swedish ambassador to the Vatican, described as a Catholic organization, in an article written to encourage Sweden's 1995 entry into the European Union, indicates that the continent of Europe is the arena of experimentation for each of these aims. Bergquist's article which was entitled, *The Way to the European Community is Via Rome,* appeared in Stokholm's premier newspaper Syd Svenska Dagbladet, October 16, 1991.

Shortly after, the Sydney Morning Herald, November, 1991, reported that John Paul II, speaking in St. Peter's Bassilica to 137 European Bishops, revealed

> his long-standing dream of a continent united on Christian (Roman Catholic) principles, from the Atlantic to the Urals, from the Mediterranean Sea to the North Pole.

The Singapore Straits Times, January 6, 1992, in an article extracted from the London Financial Times, entitled Pope Hopes to Capitalize On the Fall of Communism," reported that,

> By the millennial standards of the Holy See, Pope John Paul II is in a hurry to stamp the imprint of the Church on the fast-changing events in Europe."

The European Union's plunge into the unified currency in January 1, 1999 was a huge step towards central fiscal control of the continent. Already 11 sovereign nations of Europe; Austria, Belgium, Finland, France, Germany, Ireland, Italy, Luxemburg, Netherlands, Portugal, and Spain, have embarked on the course which will see their traditional currencies discarded by the Euro currency on July 1, 2002. Denmark, Greece, Sweden, and the United Kingdom are expected to join them shortly. It should not escape our attention that these 4 abstaining nations are non-Roman Catholic. Of the 5 predominately non-Roman Catholic nations in the European Union, only Finland was amongst those which initially joined the European Monetary Union.

The International and the European Courts of Justice are gradually welding a unified legal system, while the ecumenical movement is fast moving towards a Christianity which will be totally dominated by Rome. No other church in Christendom stands the least hope of effectively challenging Rome's will, her settled doctrines and her usurped ecclesiastical authority.

Peregrine Worsthorne, Editor of the prestigious *London Sunday Telegraph* (August 25, 1991), astutely summed up the situation in Europe, the prototype for globalism. He wrote,

> It is the movement towards federalism of the Common Market...that the Pope may see the greatest possibility for an increase in Catholic political power since the fall of Napoleon, or since the Counter-Reformation. The Common Market itself started under the influence of Catholic politicians....If European federalism triumphs, the EC (European Community) will indeed be an empire. It will lack an emperor, but it will have the Pope."

It is a small wonder that Worsthorne entitled his article, "Now, a Holy European Empire?" If the Vatican could topple Communism in Eastern Europe as asserted, quite correctly, in an article by *Time*, February 24, 1992, entitled "Holy Alliance," then it is indeed ready to conquer the world.

Dr. Malachi Martin, with remarks born of inside information, sums up the Pope's and, no doubt, the Curia's aims:

> It is not too much to say, in fact, that the chosen purpose of John Paul's pontificate—the engine that drives his papal grand policy and that determines his day-to-day, year-by-year strategies—is to be the victor in that competition, now well under way. For the fact is that the stakes John Paul has placed in the arena of geopolitical contention include everything—himself; his papal persona; the age-old Petrine Office he now embodies; and his entire Church Universal, both as an

institutional organization unparalleled in the world and as a body of believers united by a bond of mystical communion. (op. cit., p. 17)

The same author on pages 282–292 reveals that the Vatican has four Provincial Globalist groups set up in order to bring all world religions under Rome's umbrella. These embrace the following faiths:

The First Provincial Globalist Group – Islam

The Second Provincial Globalist Group – Seventh-day Adventists, Baptists, Evangelical churches, Christian Scientists, Jehovah's Witnesses, Mormons, and Unitarians.

The Third Provincial Globalist Group – Eastern Orthodox churches, and the Anglican Church.

The Fourth Provincial Globalist Group – Animism, Shintoism, Hinduism, and Buddism.

Clearly the Vatican is not only well positioned to fulfil the prophecy of Revelation 13, it has a full strategy in place to do so. We are in the last days! Only the plain word of Scripture and our adherence, in God's power, to its precepts, can keep us faithful to our Lord and His truth.

The first beast of Revelation 13 is the Papacy. No other nation has ruled for 1260 years. None other has received a deadly wound that has been so comprehensively healed. *All* the world today is wondering after the Papacy and giving deference to it. It arose from Imperial Rome. In its rise, three powerful nations were utterly obliterated. In addition, it, and it alone, fulfills or will fulfill every one of the 81 criteria of the beast power.

Already 64 of the 81 criteria have been fulfilled. The remaining 17 (see Chapter 4—criteria 6, 12, 13, 20, 50, 54, 55, 56, 59, 62, 63, 69, 74, 78, 79, 80, and 81) are yet future. We can confidently anticipate their fulfillment in view of the precise fulfillment of the other 64 criteria.

SHARED CHARACTERISTICS OF SYMBOLS OF THE BEAST	LITTLE HORN	MAN OF SIN/SON OF PERDITION	ANTICHRIST	BEAST OF REVELATION 13	BABYLON	BEAST OF REVELATION 17	THE WHORE
PERSECUTES THE SAINTS	Dan. 7:19-21, 25			Rev. 13:7, 15, 17	Rev. 17:6	Rev. 17:13, 14	Rev. 17:6
POSSESSES POWER 1260 YEARS	Dan. 7:25			Rev. 13:5			
BLASPHEMES AND OPPOSES GOD	Dan. 7:8, 25	2 Thes. 2:4	1 Jo. 2:22	Rev. 13:1, 5, 6	Rev. 17:5		Rev. 17:5
DOMINION REMOVED AT THE END OF THE WORLD	Dan. 7:26	2 Thes. 2:8		Rev. 19:20	Rev. 18:10	Rev. 17:8	Rev. 17:1
DECEPTIVE POWER		2 Thes. 2:3, 10, 11	1 Jo. 2:22 1 Jo. 4:3, 4 2 Jo. 7	Rev. 13:14	Rev. 14:8		
OPPOSES TRUE WORSHIP		2 Thes. 2:4		Rev. 13:8			
POSSESSED POWER OVER THE WORLD				Rev. 16:1, 2, 19	Rev. 14:8 Rev. 18:24 Rev. 18:3	Rev. 17:18	Rev. 17:12
RETRIBUTION FOR ALL WHO WORSHIP THE BEAST		2 Thes. 2:12		Rev. 15:2, 3	Rev. 14:9-11 Rev. 18:6, 7 Rev. 16:19	Rev. 17:15-17	
THOSE WHO REJECT THE BEAST WILL BE SAVED	Dan. 7:26		1 Jo. 2:25, 28	Rev. 20:4	Rev. 18:4		
BEAST ITSELF WILL BE WORSHIPPED		2 Thes. 2:4		Rev. 13:4, 8			
SATAN MOTIVATES BEAST		2 Thes. 2:9		Rev. 13:2	Rev. 18:2		
THE WORLD WONDERS AFTER THE BEAST				Rev. 13:3		Rev. 17:8	

MANIFESTLY, THE REFORMERS BASED THEIR IDENTIFICATION OF THE BEAST UPON SOLID BIBLICAL EVIDENCE.

Chapter 7 — The Second Beast of Revelation 13

And I beheld another beast coming up out of the earth; and he had two horns like a lamb, and he spake as a dragon (Revelation 13:11).

We have yet to identify the second beast of Revelation 13. This verse alone provides evidence of the identity of the second beast. Beasts, as we have seen, represent nations and powers. Thus the lion of Daniel 7 represented Babylon, the bear, Medo-Persia, the leopard, Greece, and the nondescript beast, Rome. The ten-horned and seven-headed beast of Revelation 13 represented the Papacy. Scripture, itself, plainly states that the four beasts of Daniel 7 represent kingdoms, as in a similar way today, a bear represents Russia, the eagle—United States, the kangaroo—Australia, and the panda—China.

Thus he said, The fourth beast shall be the fourth kingdom upon earth, which shall be diverse from all kingdoms, and shall devour the whole earth, and shall tread it down, and break it in pieces. (Daniel 7:23)

So we must search for another nation which emerged about the time that the first beast received its deadly wound (1798) for that is the time-frame of the prophecy of Revelation 13. Further, there are two points of marked distinction between the two beasts of Revelation. The first is that the papal beast arose "up out of the sea" (Revelation 13:1). In contrast, the second beast arose "up out of the earth." These contrasting origins are not inconsequential. The second contrast is that the first beast was a composite of ferocious animals — lion, bear, and leopard (Revelation 13:2). The second beast is initially represented as a gentle beast bearing "two horns like a lamb" (Revelation 13:11).

With these two marked contrasts, united with the era of its rise to power, the identity can be made. Firstly, what does sea or waters represent in the prophecies of Revelation? The meaning of the symbolism is explained in the book itself.

> And he saith unto me, The waters which thou sawest, where the whore sitteth, are peoples, and multitudes, and nations, and tongues (Revelation 17:15).

Without question the Papacy arose upon a continent which was well populated with multitudes. By contrast the second beast, in arising from the earth, was to emerge in a continent sparsely populated. Were any nations emerging in underpopulated continents around 1798? Yes, there were two. In 1776, a small nation of three million people, largely confined to the east coast of a large continent, won its independence from the United Kingdom. Of course that nation was the United States. Twenty-two years later it was still in the preliminary stages of forging its destiny. The other nation was Australia which commenced as a convict settlement precisely a decade prior to the inflicting of the "deadly wound." Both these nations arose in sparsely populated continents. In 1798, Australia's white population was still counted in the thousands. When the white convicts and their penal guards arrived ten years earlier, there was an estimate of 300,000 - 500,000 aboriginals thinly spread over the almost 3,000,000 square miles (more than 7,000,000 square kilometers) of the continent.

However, the prophecy leaves us in no doubt as to which of these two nations fitted the prophetic depiction. The Papacy arose as a fierce power. Its brutal treatment of religious dissenters and its pursuit of its political agenda leave no cause to deny the representation as a ferocious beast. The United States arose in a gentle atmosphere. The two horns of the lamb could aptly symbolize its establishment of both religious and civil liberties.

No penal colony, like Australia, with its cruel exactions upon prisoners, could possibly have been described in terms of a lamb. It may not have had the ferocious history of the Papacy, but it most certainly was no lamb either. But further, as we study the future history of the second beast, it must be a nation possessing enormous worldwide influence and power. Here the United States stands unchallenged.

Let us examine the dire prophecies concerning this second beast. It has already been seen that he was later to speak as a dragon. The Bible explains who the dragon is.

> And the great dragon was cast out, that old serpent, called the Devil, and Satan, which deceiveth the whole world: he was cast out into the earth, and his angels were cast out with him (Revelation 12:9).

This is curious. The United States has been recognized as a Christian nation, seeking to inculcate Christian values into the society. But this prophecy is too plain to ignore. It will alter this noble course and rather do a work contrary to God's will.

We are told what that work will be.

> And he exerciseth all the power of the first beast before him, and causeth the earth and them which dwell therein to worship the first beast, whose deadly wound was healed (Revelation 13:12).

Here, once more, we notice that the issue at stake is worship. With its worldwide influence, the United States will exert similar coercive means used by the historic Papacy to enforce the agenda of the Papacy. The Apostolic Letter of May 28, 1998, *Ad Tuendum Fidem,* which introduces a number of new punitive canons should leave no doubt that the Papacy has once more considered the need to punish heretics. We must not lose sight of the fact that the penalties were unspecified and the recipients of such penalties were equally undefined ("whoever" and "a person").

Clearly, remarkable miracles will be performed by the second beast and these will be urged as evidence that the movement to support the aims of the Papacy is God-ordained. We must never forget that Satan is perfectly capable of performing certain miracles, as occurred when Moses and Aaron appeared before Pharaoh.

> And he doeth great wonders, so that he maketh fire come down from heaven on the earth in the sight of men, And deceiveth them that dwell on the earth, by the means of those miracles which he had power to do in the sight of the beast; saying to them that dwell on the earth, that they should make an image to the beast, which had the wound by a sword, and did live (Revelation 13:13,14).

The ability to call fire down from heaven will be compelling evidence to many imperceptive Christians that the support of the papal agenda is the work of God. The example of Elijah upon Mount Carmel is bound to be recalled. In that case God manifestly prevented Satan from counterfeiting the divine miracle. But, in a test of mankind's fidelity to Scripture as the only certain guide to truth, Satan will, in the last days, counterfeit the working of God through Elijah on Mount Carmel.

The popularity of the ecumenical movement in the United States, as in other nations, is bound to serve as a spearhead for the American simulation of papal methods, power, and aims as it develops its "image to the beast." Every thinking individual knows full well that one Christian sect alone will ultimately benefit from the ecumenical thrust and that is the Roman Catholic Church. To this common sense observation the Bible fully attests. So successful will this movement be that all but a small, dedicated group of Christians will unite in the single religion forged by the Papacy and enforced by American might. After all, the proven most successful evangelistic technique has been the enactment of severe penalties imposed upon dissenters. It is amazing how many, devoid of genuine conviction, will come to heel under such conditions.

Such laws will be legislated as we shall see. Both an economic boycott and the death penalty will be imposed upon those who refuse to accept the observance of the papal Sabbath.

> And he had power to give life unto the image of the beast, that the image of the beast should both speak, and cause that as many as would not worship the image of the beast should be killed. And he causeth all, both small and great, rich and poor, free and bond, to receive a mark in their right hand, or in their foreheads: And that no man might buy or sell, save he that had the mark, or the name of the beast, or the number of his name (Revelation 13:15-17).

Many will refuse to accept the plain evidence of Scripture, but as the days roll by they will see that God's word will not be mocked. It is certain and it will be fulfilled. Presently a great wave of Sunday laws are being promoted around the world. On April 4, 1998 the city of Bendigo in Australia held a Sunday-law referendum promoted by the Roman Catholic, Anglican, Presbyterian, and Uniting Church of Australia (a union of Methodists, Congregationalists, and a segment of Presbyterians) (*Melbourne Sunday Herald,* Sunday, April 5, 1998). In the Netherlands in March 1998, the Netherlands Council of Churches promoted a petition to the Government of the Netherlands, pushing for the enactment of a single day of worship for all. On March 1, 1998 the Lincoln *Sunday Journal Star* reported the discussions in the Nebraska State Senate on the subject of a Sunday rest day. Incredibly, Pakistan, a nation of 120,000,000 citizens, 95 percent of whom adhere to the Islamic faith, altered its rest day from Friday to Sunday on April 1, 1997 (*Deccan Herald,* April 2, 1997). In 1998

Norway, with bipartisan political support, enacted a Sunday rest day.

Almost all of these moves have been supported on the grounds that we need a social day — a day for the family, for relaxation, for rest. But behind such admirable aims is a religious agenda. Why is it necessary for any government to force a rest day, selected by it, upon its citizens? Governments possess the prerogative to recommend health measures to their citizens, but the principle of civil liberty surely demands that the citizen has the right to accept or reject the advice. As for selecting a specific day and enforcing it, even if the majority of citizens acquiesce, this is a breach of both civil and even more importantly, religious liberty. It should be resisted by all clear-thinking citizens.

The campaign of the churches in Bendigo, Australia was named "Save Our Sundays." The four major religious sects which promoted this Sunday law referendum chose a particularly inappropriate slogan. Every convicted Sunday-keeper is entitled to the free exercise of his faith — that is true religious liberty. However, in Bendigo there was no move to restrict Sunday-keeping. Ever since the city was founded 150 years ago, convicted Sunday-keepers have been afforded the right to worship in their churches on Sunday, to close their businesses on Sunday, to refrain from shopping on Sunday, and to educated their children on days other than Sunday. There was nothing from which to save Sunday. The real aim of the campaign of this ecumenical combination of Roman Catholics and Protestants was to impose their convictions upon those who did not share with them these identical convictions. It was a direct effort to withdraw religious liberty from one section of the populace. Fortunately, when such matters were brought to the attention of the city's citizenry they rejected the proposal by a 78 percent "No" vote. But Scripture indicates that it will not always be so.

Fueling the Sunday-law movement are the apparitions of Mary. In the United States a report of an apparition of Mary has received widespread circulation. A video tape, entitled *Prophecy and the New Times**, documenting numerous appearances and what she said, has found a ready reception in the United States. She has been quoted as having warned of dire disasters coming upon the United States. She assured Americans that she is desirous of pleading with our Heavenly Father to stay these natural catastrophes. However there is an impediment to the positive response to her plea. This impediment, she asserts, is the failure to keep Sunday holy. She refers to four matters which require rectification — shopping on Sundays, the playing of competitive sports on Sundays, absence from Mass, and failure to attend confession. When these breaches of Sunday sacredness are corrected, Mary has assured Americans that our Heavenly Father is sure to hold back these fearful disasters.

Christ has warned of fearful natural disasters at the end of time. He told His disciples that famines, pestilences, and earthquakes would occur (Matthew 24:7). Mary's warning, therefore, is certain to be fulfilled, and is presently in the process of being fulfilled to a limited extent.

Mary "believers" are all too ready to accept Mary's warning as messages from God. In the minds of many, the fact that Satan is capable of deception is rarely considered. Yet on four occasions Jesus, in His discourse on last-day events, warned against deceptions (Matthew 24:4, 5, 11, 24). Indeed, the last of these verses warns that the deceptions will be so great that they, if it were possible, would deceive the very elect.

How may humans decide if an apparition is godly or a satanic deception? The Bible provides one sure way.

> To the law and to the testimony: if they speak not according to this word, it is because there is no light in them (Isaiah 8:20).

* Available from Hartland Publications, P.O. Box 1, Rapidan, VA 22733, USA, Telephone: 1-800-774-3566. In Australia, PO Box 175, Kalorama, Victoria 3766, Australia, Telephone: 03-9751-1932

Thus the Bible is the only sure guide. So let us judge these apparitions of Mary by this criterion.

Firstly, we know that Mary is dead, so let us review the testimony of Scripture on this subject. The Bible refers to death as a sleep, not as an alert condition.

> And why dost thou not pardon my transgression, and take away mine iniquity? for now shall I sleep in the dust; and thou shalt seek me in the morning, but I shall not be (Job 7:21).

> But man dieth, and wasteth away: yea, man giveth up the ghost, and where is he? As the waters fail from the sea, and the flood decayeth and drieth up: So man lieth down, and riseth not: till the heavens be no more, they shall not awake, nor be raised out of their sleep. O that thou wouldest hide me in the grave, that thou wouldest keep me secret, until thy wrath be past, that thou wouldest appoint me a set time, and remember me! (Job 14:10-13).

> These things said he: and after that he saith unto them, Our friend Lazarus sleepeth; but I go, that I may awake him out of sleep. Then said his disciples, Lord, if he sleep, he shall do well. Howbeit Jesus spake of his death: but they thought that he had spoken of taking of rest in sleep. Then said Jesus unto them plainly, Lazarus is dead (John 11: 11-14).

> And the graves were opened; and many bodies of the saints which slept arose, And came out of the graves after his resurrection, and went into the holy city, and appeared unto many (Matthew 27: 52,53).

The Scriptures also declare that the dead know nothing.

> For the living know that they shall die: but the dead know not any thing, neither have they any more a reward; for the memory of them is forgotten. Also their love, and their hatred, and their envy, is now perished; neither have they any more a portion for ever in any thing that is done under the sun....Whatsoever thy hand findeth to do, do it with thy might; for there is no work, nor device, nor knowledge, nor wisdom, in the grave, whither thou goest. (Ecclesiastes 9:5-6,10).

> His sons came to honour, and he knoweth it not; and they are brought

low, but he perceiveth it not of them (Job 14:21).

For in death there is no remembrance of thee: in the grave who shall give thee thanks? (Psalms 6:5).

The dead praise not the Lord, neither any that go down into silence (Psalms 115:17).

His breath goeth forth, he returneth to his earth; in that very day his thoughts perish (Psalms 146:4).

The entire focus of Scripture is that the righteous dead are raised to eternal life at the second coming of Christ.

Looking for that blessed hope, and the glorious appearing of the great God and our Saviour Jesus Christ (Titus 2:13)

Behold, I shew you a mystery; We shall not all sleep, but we shall all be changed, In a moment, in the twinkling of an eye, at the last trump: for the trumpet shall sound, and the dead shall be raised incorruptible, and we shall be changed (1 Corinthians 15: 51,52)

But I would not have you ignorant my brethren, concerning them which are asleep, that ye sorrow not, even as others which have no hope. For if we believe that Jesus died and rose again, even so them also which sleep in Jesus will God bring with him. For this we say unto you by the word of the Lord, that we which are alive and remain unto the coming of the Lord shall not prevent them which are asleep. For the Lord himself shall descend from heaven with a shout, with the voice of the archangel, and with the trump of God: and the dead in Christ shall rise first: Then we which are alive and remain shall be caught up together with them in the clouds, to meet the Lord in the air: and so shall we ever be with the Lord. Wherefore comfort one another with these words (1 Thessalonians 4: 13-18).

Since Mary is dead she knows nothing and possesses no thoughts. She is "asleep" in Jesus, awaiting His return and the resurrection. Then the Mary of the apparitions is manifestly a deception. No matter how sweet and loving she may appear, no matter how elevated her speech, she is the result of spiritism. Satan is the master impersonator. He impersonated Samuel when King Saul visited the witch of Endor.

We further know that the counterfeit Mary of the apparitions is not of God, for she advocates Sunday worship, the external mark of the beast. The state of man in death is a crucial matter, for we will surely be deceived by the devil if we do not accept the plain Bible truth that we "sleep" in death until the second coming of Christ.*

But those unacquainted with the Scriptural teaching of man's state in death will be subject to the subtle deceptions of Satan and prone to accept Mary's apparitions as genuine. Thus many Protestants will be deceived. Of course, Satan has read Scripture, no doubt many times. He is certainly acquainted with Christ's prophecy and uses it to his own advantage. Those who have not sought God's truth by personal Bible study will accept the natural catastrophes as the events of which the counterfeit Mary spoke, rather than signs stated to us by our Lord just prior to His crucifixion.

It is almost certain that, in desperation, unconverted people will turn to God seeking His protection and praying for Him to halt the catastrophes. Devoid of conversion, such folk are bound to become frenzied in their despair. With no successful result from their prayers they are almost certain to turn upon sabbathkeepers, judging them to be the cause of God's failure to remove the natural disasters from their midst. The implementation of legislated penalties for breach of Sunday observance would then achieve great support from the majority. It is even possible that the counterfeit Mary will point to sabbathkeepers as the cause of the continued catastrophes.

Many will point to the fact that all western nations, the United States excepted, have discarded the death penalty and thus the death decree of Revelation 13:15 cannot be universal. Such should remember that those who outlawed the death penalty can equally reenact it.

* The authors have published a book on this subject — *The Mystery of Death*, Hartland Publications, P.O. Box 1, Rapidan, VA 22733, USA, Telephone: 1-800-774-3566. In Australia, PO Box 175, Kalorama, Victoria 3766, Australia, Telephone: 03-9751-1932

Also, in some countries such as the United Kingdom, the death penalty has not been revoked for treason. Thus when nations are facing ruin as a result of natural disasters of major dimensions, it is possible that legislators, convinced that sabbathkeepers are the cause of their plight, will charge these faithful souls with treason.

The close association of the call to Mass with the Pope's call to Sunday observance causes us to ponder whether participation in the blasphemous service of the Mass will be demanded. This could well be. Many Protestants would freely concur with such a command in a period of major peril, for their leaders in Lima, Peru, in 1977, at a World Council of Churches Conference entitled Baptism, Eucharist, and Mission (BEM), agreed that all forms of communion were equally acceptable.

Yet martyrs yielded their lives rather than participate in what they regarded as the blasphemy of the Mass. Many Protestants are unaware of the claims made by the Roman Catholic Church in respect of the Mass. The Mass is indeed verification of the characteristic of blasphemy cited in Daniel 7:8,25; 2 Thessalonians 2:4; 1 John 2:22; Revelation 13:1,5,6; and Revelation 17:5.

Two blasphemous claims stand out. The Papacy claims that in the Mass, the priest becomes the creator of his Creator. Since human beings cannot create life and Christ was never created, this is a preposterous claim.

> If the person of the Redeemer had not yet been in the world, the priest by pronouncing the words of consecration would produce this great person of a Man-God. 'O wonderful dignity of the priests,' cries out Saint Augustine, 'in their hands, as in the womb of the Blessed Virgin, the son of God becomes incarnate.' Hence the priests are called the parents of Jesus Christ .... Thus the priest may, in a certain manner, be called the creator of his Creator....' 'He that created me without me, is Himself created by me' (Alphonus de Liguori, *Dignity and Duties of the Priest,* pp. 32,33, New York, Benziger Brothers, 1888).

Further still, the sacrifice of Christ on Calvary is equated to the Mass. This is blasphemy indeed!

> The Eucharistic sacrifice is to be considered in so far that in it Christ offers Himself, that is, He is not only the sacrificial gift, but also the most eminent Sacrificer. In this respect the sacrifice of the Mass is not inferior in value to that of the cross: both are equally [infinite], equally beyond estimation and equally valuable (Dr. Nicholas Gihr, *The Holy Sacrifice of the Mass,* English Edition, 1939, B. Herder Book Co., St. Louis and London, p. 135 — this book received the Imprimatur of Archbishop Gleeson of St. Louis).

True Protestants will never yield to participating in such blasphemy. Rather would they be faithful unto death (Revelation 2:10). But as the Protestants of the United States and other nations become more and more embroiled in the web of ecumenism, they are positioning themselves to be deceived by the artifices of the first beast of Revelation 13, and placing themselves in the role of the second beast.

Chapter 8 — The United States and Religious Liberty

W hen Roger Williams, the founder of the state of Rhode Island, included a guarantee of religious liberty in the Constitution of that state, it became the first state ever to do so. This led to the first Sabbath-keeper migrating to the United States. In 1664, Stephen Mumford arrived in Rhode Island. He had fled his native England fearing the same fate as John James who three years earlier, in 1661, had refused to cease preaching on the Sabbath day, at the command of the sheriffs of King Charles II. He was convicted of high treason and hanged, drawn, and quartered. Mumford spread his convictions and eventually the Seventh Day Baptist church was established in America.

Roger Williams had himself been banished from Massachusetts in 1631 because he

> had declared his opinion that the magistrate might not punish a breach of the Sabbath (Sunday) *Winthrop's Journal,* Vol. 1, pp. 52,53, cited in *American State Papers,* Third Edition, p. 57, Review and Herald Publishing Association, 1943.

Despite the fact that a large number of immigrants arriving in the United States during its founding days were escaping religious persecution themselves, they afforded little religious liberty to those who were of minority faiths within their own borders. Many of the original states breached the religious liberties of citizens who desired only to worship God as their consciences dictated. The Congregational Church in Massachusetts, the Methodists in Kansas, and the Church of England (Episcopalian) in Virginia had particularly poor records of religious liberty in the early days, and even the early Quaker settlers in Pennsylvania were not convinced of the concept of religious liberty in their colony.

The inclusion of the guarantee of religious liberty and the separation of church and state into the First Amendment of the United States Constitution was a great step forward in the provision of religious liberty for the citizens of the United States. Yet over and over again it failed to prevent the states from enacting and enforcing Sunday laws in the nineteenth century. The record of the United States in that century was poor. Many virtuous persons were jailed, even placed in chain gangs or ruined financially, simply because they failed to desist from work on Sunday.

In the 1880's, Senator Blair of New Hampshire promoted Sunday legislation in the U.S. Senate with great vigor, but without success. However, it was in the nineteenth century that the ground was laid by the judiciary of the United States to open the way for widespread Sunday laws, despite the protection of religious liberty afforded under the First Amendment. Indeed, the ingenuity of the proponents of Sunday legislation in the judiciary knew no bounds in their desire to enforce such laws by circumventing the First Amendment. This should be a lesson to all Americans today.

Many believe that before Sunday laws are once more placed in force, that it would be necessary to undertake the very difficult process of repealing the First Amendment. But the history of the nineteenth century stands as a testimony that, with no little guile, the justices of various courts, were able to distort fact and claim that Sunday laws were not religious in nature. Such claims may convince the unthinking, but in reality are simply self-serving subterfuges to circumvent the clear intent of the First Amendment.

Chief Justice Stephen Field of the California Supreme Court, had, in 1858, prior to his elevation to the highest judicial post in the state, introduced a sham reasoning to ease the way for decisions in favor of Sunday legislation. As attorney Warren Johns states,

> Field, aware that Sunday laws rested on shaky ground if justification was tied to religious purposes... offered constitutional refuge to blue laws [Sunday laws] by treating them as civil rather than religious legislation (Warren Johns, *Dateline Sunday,* Pacific Press, 1963, pp. 84,85).

Since Field was later elevated to the Supreme Court of the United States, his legal ploy was carried into that court. Field asserted that health and welfare benefits would result from a weekly rest day. This form of promotion has now surfaced in countries such as Australia, the Netherlands, and Norway. In Nebraska, the move for a Sunday law was rooted on the grounds that it made the state "family friendly" (Lincoln *Sunday Journal Star,* March 1, 1998). Further as we have seen, the Pope's Apostolic Letter, *Dies Domini,* has advocated Sunday civil legislation on the grounds of its benefits for servants and workers. But a serious student of these moves to Sunday legislation will not be deceived. They are religious, strictly religious. The fact that the moves arise from Roman Catholic and Protestant sources should deceive no one. Make no mistake, the chief victims of Sunday law enforcement have always been religious minorities. It must not escape the notice of the wise that although civil penalties have been invoked for breaches of Sunday laws, no such penalties have been enacted for failure to rest on civil rest days such as national holidays. When was anyone prosecuted for failure to rest on the fourth of July or Martin Luther King day? If a government believes that at least one day of rest is essential per week for all citizens, what purpose can there be in confining that day to Sunday? Surely the citizen should be afforded the privilege of choosing such a day at his convenience. Does a rest on Sunday ensure better health than a rest on Monday? The answer is that all Sunday laws proscribing labor are religious and in the United States do breach the First Amendment of the American Constitution.

Even as recently as 1932,

> A deputy sheriff [in Virginia] arrested two Seventh-day Adventists for Sunday work, one — a crippled mother who walked on crutches — for washing clothes on her own premises, and the other, a man who donated and hauled a load of wood to church to heat it for religious services (*American State Papers,* op. cit., p. 567).

In 1926 a spy saw a man pressing his trousers on Sunday in Baltimore, Maryland. He was fined. In Georgia in 1930, police arrested a Bible colporteur for delivering a book of Bible exposition on Sunday, yet assisted a circus to set up and permitted an airplane to give joy rides on the very same day (Warren Johns, op. cit., p. 114). We need not be deceived. Sunday laws are aimed primarily against **religious dissenters.** Numerous other such cases are extant and have been documented in Warren Johns' masterly book.

The history of the enacting of religious laws by governments, the union of church and state, is a very explosive one. Inevitably, such legislation leads to deprivation of religious liberty and persecution of minorities. Governments possess one right and one right alone in religious matters — the protection of the religious liberty of all their citizens. Happy is the nation where the government confines its religious legislation to that single prerogative.

Rightly, in 1959, the Federal Court found that the Massachusetts Sunday laws were religious. But in 1962, the Supreme Court of the United States ruled by an 8-1 majority that Sunday laws did not breach the First Amendment. This was an incredible decision and a most dangerous one. This decision has not been revoked or over-turned. It stands ready for and favorable to the enactment of Sunday laws. The First Amendment has proved to be little protection, in these last days, against the promotion of the sectarian convictions of the majority and the revoking of religious liberty of all. The United States stands well-positioned to assist the first beast power in enforcing Sunday observance.

In presenting the majority decision, Chief Justice Earl Warren claimed that

> ...to say that states cannot prescribe Sunday as a day of rest for these [secular] purposes solely because centuries ago such laws had their genesis in religion would give a Constitutional interpretation of hostility to the public welfare rather than one of mere separation of church and state.

He went on to write,

> It is common knowledge that the first day of the week has come to have special significance as a day of rest in this country. People of all religions and people of no religion regard Sunday as a time for family activity, for visiting friends and relatives, for late sleeping, for passive and active entertainment, for dining out and the like.... Sunday is a day apart from all others. The cause is irrelevant; the fact exists. It would seem unrealistic to require a state to choose a common day of rest other than that most persons would select of their own accord (Case *McGowan v. Maryland*).

Despite the assertion of this eminent jurist, the cause is most decidedly *not* irrelevant. The cause denotes a sorry history of religious persecution. In any case, what business is it of a state to enforce any day as a day of rest for all citizens?

Justice Felix Frankfurter also wrote an opinion in this case, in support of the majority decision. He implausibly acknowledged that

> ...the earlier among the colonial statutes were unquestionably religious in purpose.... But even the seventeenth century legislation does not show an exclusive religious preoccupation.

Only Justice William Douglas dissented in the four Sunday law cases adjudged in 1961 (*Gallagher v. Crown Kosher Supermarket; McGowan v. Maryland; Two Guys from Harrison v. McGinley; Brownfeld v. Brown).* Justice Douglas asserted, quite properly, in his dissenting opinion that Sunday laws did in fact breach both the establishment clause (that is, the prohibition of the State establishing a religion) and the free exercise clause (the right of all citizens to exercise their faith freely) as enshrined in the First Amendment. He well stated that

> The First Amendment commands government to have no interest in theology or ritual; it admonishes government to be interested in allowing religious freedom to flourish — whether the result is to produce Catholics, Jews or Protestants, or to turn the people toward the path of Buddha, or to end in a predominately Moslem nation, or to produce in the long run atheists or agnostics!

In citing the protection of the religious liberty of all citizens, Justice Douglas expressed a dictum of great wisdom.

But Justice Douglas' opinion, expressed so cogently and with great wisdom, did not prevail. Americans remain under the judicial imposition that Sunday laws do not breach the First Amendment, despite the fact that they clearly do.

In recent years two other major decisions of the Supreme Court have further positioned the United States to fulfill the actions of the second beast of Revelation, while God does not predestinate, He does foresee the future with equal clarity as He does the past and present.

On April 17, 1990 in the case of *Smith v. the State of Oregon,* the Supreme Court by a 5-4 majority effectively removed the religious liberty of every citizen. The case itself is not so much of interest. It concerned American Indians who treated fellow American Indians for various ailments including drug abuse. They were employed by the State of Oregon. It was discovered that these health workers were themselves taking a drug, peyote, in pagan religious rites to which they adhered. Consequently the state fired them. They ultimately appealed to the Supreme Court, claiming that their First Amendment rights had been breached.

They lost the case. What did concern those who value religious liberty was that in his majority opinion

> Justice Antonin Scalia went far beyond the case and declared that when religious rights clash with the government's need for uniform rules, the court will side with the government (*Los Angeles Times,* April 18, 1990).

In commenting the newspaper stated,

> the Supreme Court Tuesday forcefully declared that it would no longer shield believers whose practices violate general laws (Ibid.).

Following the Civil War, the Fourteenth Amendment had been added to the United States Constitution. It stated in part, that

> No state shall make or enforce any law which shall abridge the privileges or immunities of citizens of the United States; nor shall any State deprive any person of life, liberty, or property, without due process of law, nor deny to any person within its jurisdiction the equal protection of the laws.

The Amendment, as time passed, was interpreted to protect citizens from state legislation which was in

> ...conflict with the United States Constitution. By 1925 the United States Supreme Court had decreed that First Amendment guarantees were applicable to state and local government through the provisions of the Fourteenth Amendment (Warren Johns, op. cit., p. 113).

Such support of the First Amendment by the Fourteenth Amendment led the Supreme Court, in the 1940's, to uphold the right of Jehovah's Witnesses refusing to salute the flag. In 1986 the Supreme Court told the states that they

> ...could not deny unemployment benefits to Seventh-day Adventists who refused to work on Saturdays (*Los Angeles Times,* April 18,

1990).

In 1972, the U.S. Supreme Court exempted Amish children from compulsory school laws.

But subsequently, the 1990 Smith decision was antagonistic to all such decisions. Justice Sandra Day O'Connor, presenting the dissenting opinion of the four Supreme Court justices who objected to Justice Scalia's opinion, (even though she herself was one of the six justices who denied the Smith claim for reinstatement), stated that Justice Scalia's opinion

> ...is incompatible with our nation's commitment to individual religious liberty. In my view, the First Amendment was enacted precisely to protect the rights of those whose religious practices are not shared by the majority and may be viewed with hostility (*Los Angeles Times,* April 18, 1990).

In this opinion, Justice O'Connor was absolutely correct. The majority decision was an affront to religious liberty in the United States.

President Bill Clinton attempted to redress the issue through legislating a bill to restore religious liberty and although it passed Congress, it was struck down by the Supreme Court.

Did the *Smith v. the State of Oregon* decision have practical implications in respect of the deprivation of religious liberty of American citizens? Most definitely it did. Those effects were rapid. Only just over ten months later, the *Washington Post,* March 9, 1991, listed numbers of cases where citizens were deprived of their religious liberty by the court's majority opinion in the *Smith* case.

The most glaring example is that of the *Yang* case. The Yang family had migrated to the United States from Laos. They were Buddhists. Tragically their 23-year-old son died of natural causes. The physician requested an autopsy, but the parents refused permission since the Buddhist faith opposes such procedures. Ignoring the parents' prohibition, the physicians performed the post-mortem. The

Yangs sought compensation on the grounds that "the forced autopsy infringed on their religious freedom" (Ibid.). In January, 1990, U.S. District Judge Raymond J. Pettine upheld their claim. We observe that this decision was delivered three months *prior* to the Smith decision of the Supreme Court. No decision was made at that time in respect of damages. Ten months later, when Pettine was deciding how much money the family should be awarded, the judge announced "with deep regret" and "the deepest sympathy for the Yangs" — that the Smith decision had forced him to reverse his ruling" (Ibid.).

The Yangs clearly had been deprived of their religious liberty by the Smith decision. Their claim had been upheld three months before that decision and negated seven months after the decision. Ironically this decision was taken in the state of Rhode Island, where Roger Williams had been the seventeenth-century trailblazer in guaranteeing religious liberty to its citizens.

A Jewish woman in Michigan lost a similar case under the Smith decision when an autopsy was performed on her son. The Jewish faith forbids autopsies. A Moslem prison inmate in Illinois lost his petition to be served a diet devoid of pork on the same grounds (Ibid.). Numbers of other cases were listed. The Smith decision did override the First Amendment protections and thus made it almost ineffectual. The United States has virtually reached the stage of the incredible decision of the Supreme Court of the State of New Jersey which found, in the case, *State of New Jersey v. Perricones (1962),* that "the freedom of religion guaranteed in the First Amendment to the United States Constitution was the freedom of belief, not the freedom of practice, and religious practices could be controlled by the state" (Montie Barringer, *Insight,* August 2, 1977). To provide the right of belief but not of practice is to provide only that liberty which cannot be taken from the individual, for it is a matter of the mind.

Referring to the Smith case, Forest Montgomery, counsel for the National Association of Evangelicals stated that

...the problem with the [Smith] decision is that the United States Supreme Court has gutted the free exercise of the First Amendment (*Washington Post,* March 9, 1991).

Thus the Supreme Court has now put in place a decision which would permit the government, if it felt a compelling reason to do so, to trample the consciences of sabbathkeepers.

Further, on March 26, 1991, the Supreme Court removed the protection afforded under the Fifth Amendment of the U.S. Constitution. The case concerned the death penalty imposed upon Oreste Fulminante by an Arizona court. Fulminante had

...confessed murder of his 11-year-old stepdaughter to a fellow inmate working as a government informant (*Washington Post,* March 27, 1991).

He appealed to the Supreme Court on the grounds that his confession was coerced. By a 5-4 majority, the Supreme Court held that Fulminante's confession had been coerced and his appeal was upheld. One would have thought that the result would simply have been that the trial verdict would be quashed and a new trial would be called at which the confession would have been inadmissable. However, the justices once more went far beyond the case itself and

...voted that some convictions may be allowed to stand despite the case of confessions obtained *in violation of the defendant's constitutional rights* (Ibid., emphasis supplied).

The Fifth Amendment guarantees that no coerced confession is admissable evidence of guilt in a trial. This has been interpreted to include psychological coercion as well as physical torture. In writing the majority opinion, Chief Justice William Rehnquist spoke of "harmless error" in admitting such evidence before a court. It is difficult to describe the use of a coerced confession as harmless. One of the justices, Anthony Kennedy, credibly stated that

...other than a videotape of the crime one would have difficulty in finding evidence more damaging to a criminal plea of innocence than a confession (Ibid.).

It seems unconscionable that Supreme Court justices boldly state that "the use of confessions in violation of the defendant's constitutional rights" is sometimes acceptable in a criminal case. Decisions such as this place the judiciary above the Constitution, to which they should be subject.

It is little wonder that Justice Byron White, writing for the dissenting justices stated that,

Permitting a coerced confession which could be part of the evidence on which a jury is free to bare its verdict of guilty is incompatible with the thesis that ours is not an *inquisitional* system of criminal justice (Ibid., emphasis added).

White's use of the word "inquisitional" was perfectly justifiable for surely all use of coercion in order to extract a confession harks back to the days of the inquisition.

The Jewish system of justice two thousand years ago accepted no confession of guilt as evidence in criminal trials. This judicial rule applied whether the accused was subject to coercion or freely made such a confession. This was a wonderful protection for often it is difficult to prove a confession to be coerced. While at Christ's trial Caiaphas in desperation used Christ's confession that He was the Son of God in order to convict Him of blasphemy, he did so in breach of the Jewish law.

But Jesus held his peace. And the high priest answered and said unto him, I adjure thee by the living God, that thou tell us whether thou be the Christ, the Son of God. Jesus saith unto him, Thou hast said: nevertheless I say unto you, Hereafter shall ye see the Son of man sitting on the right hand of power, and coming in the clouds of heaven. Then the high priest rent his clothes, saying, He hath spoken blasphemy; what further need have we of witnesses? Behold, now ye have heard his blasphemy (Matthew 26:63-65).

Chapter 9 — The United States is Positioned to Enforce Religious Compliance with Papal Desires

Time magazine February 24, 1992 in its cover story, "The Holy Alliance," demonstrated how closely the United States and the Vatican worked together in order to engineer the demise of communism in Eastern Europe. Of course communism was an evil political system. Nevertheless, citizens of those nations were encouraged to act as intelligence agents for the Vatican /United States covert operations. President Ronald Reagan appeared to be oblivious to the fact that the same system of laymen, priests, bishops, archbishops, and cardinals is to be found in the United States. While many of these Roman Catholics are no doubt fiercely loyal to their homeland, many also possess an understandable primary loyalty to their faith and readily comply with the desires of the Vatican.

"Baptist open to Ties With Catholics," proclaimed a headline in *The Columbus Dispatch*, Ohio, June 17, 1994. The reference was to the Southern Baptist Church, America's largest Protestant church. The International Herald-Tribune, June 27, 1998, headlined, "Catholics and Lutherans Settle a Historic Doctrinal Dispute." Since the doctrine under discussion was that which fired the Reformation— Justification by Faith—it would seem thta Rome is making giant strides towards subduing the opposition of Protestants to its unscriptural faith.

Such success has opened the pathway to the Christian Coalition in the Unitited States where conservative Roman Catholics and Evangelical Protestants have united to promote this political agendas, thus preparing the United States to use political and judicial power to enforce Rome's eccliastical will.

The Protestant Moral Majority in the United States and its alliance with Roman Catholic conservatives may appear to be a wise conjunction of forces, designed to promote a political agenda aimed at raising the moral standards of the nation. But it is a union bound to fulfill the role of the United States prophesied in Revelation 13:11-18. Its claim that desirable matters such as the equal rights of Afro-Americans were obtained by legislative and judicial means and enforcements, therefore spiritual values may be similarly uplifted in society, may appear persuasive to some who have not studied the history of the use of the state to enforce religious convictions. However, such moves can only result in persecution of dedicated believers of different convictions. It is a pathway to disaster.

The Pope aims to control the world, especially focusing on the United States. In this he fulfils Bible prophecy. He seeks to utilize the Virgin Mary as his vehicle, even though she is dead (see the book, *The Mystery of Death*, by the same authors, Hartland Publications, 800-774-3566).

"The Holy Father longs to visit the United States one more time...." Monsignor Stanislaw Dziwisz, the Pope's private secretary and long-time friend and collaborator, says behind John Paul II's longing to see America again is his wish to honor the Blessed Virgin, to urge Americans to turn to her and to dramatically and symbolically link the great Western democracy more closely to her. "I have no doubt he would go," said Dziwisz in a conversation with *Inside the Vatican*, "if his pilgrimage could be related to some Marian occasion...." It's apparent the Vatican, aware also of the grave moral and spiritual crisis America is facing, is groping for a way to reach America, through Mary, for the Gospel....Much has been made of the need to consecrate Russia to Mary's immaculate heart. But the need to consecrate America to Mary is now just as great—perhaps greater. (*Inside the Vatican*, Roman Catholic Periodical, Editorial May, 1997).

The Pope's proclamation, released on November 29, 1998, in respect of the year 2000, is yet a further effort to expand his influence to the United States and worldwide.

In a papal bull (the highest level of Papal communication) entitled "Incarnationis Mysterium" [Mystery of the Incarnation], Pope John Paul II proclaimed 2000 a Holy Year, and issued edicts that serve as a practical guide to spiritual salvation during the Jubilee. The Pope announced in the document Friday that throughout the millennium celebration, penitents who do a charitable deed or give up cigarettes or alcohol for a day can earn an "indulgence" that will eliminate time in purgatory. (*International Herald-Tribune*, Nov. 29, 1998)

The doctrines of the practice of issuing indulgences and purgatory were major unscriptural doctrines which largely contributed to the great schism in Christianity in the sixteenth century. But the Pope has been testing the waters during 1998 and has found them very friendly. In the current ecumenical climate, a climate conducive to the benefit of the Roman Catholic Church and no other, he believes that at the commencement of the twenty-first century, these doctrines, formerly so abhorrent to Protestants, will draw them near in their pathway back to Rome.

But by broadening the ways believers can earn an indulgence beyond traditional Catholic rituals [such as attending mass, performing the stations of the cross, and saying the Rosary], the Pope is also trying to imbue indulgences with some of the *ecumenical spirit* he wants to lend the celebrations (Ibid. - emphasis supplied).

In this aim he will only succeed if Protestants so permit. The prophecies of Revelation Chapter 13 are fulfilling before our very eyes. It is surely time for Christians of all faiths to be alert lest they be deceived, to their eternal peril.

Protestants should realize the Pope stated in his Bull that,

> Participation in the Eucharist [the Mass], which is required for all indulgences, should properly take place on the same day as the prescribed works are performed. (Papal Bull *Incarnationis Mysterium*, issued November 29, 1998.)

Many Protestant martyrs died rather than partake of the blasphemy of the Mass. The Roman Catholic Church makes a number of unscriptural claims concerning the Mass.

1. It is equally valuable as the cross of Christ.

2. That the priest can create his Creator.

3. That even if Christ had not come to the earth the participation in the Mass would have been sufficient.

Read carefully the following quotations from approved Roman Catholic books on the subject. These passages appear also in Chapter 7, but we repeat them in order to emphasize their significance.

> The Eucharistic sacrifice [the Mass] is to be considered in so far as in it Jesus Christ offers Himself, that is, He is not only the sacrificial gift, but also the most eminent sacrificer. In this respect *the Sacrifice of the Mass is not inferior in value to that of the Cross*: both are equally infinite, equally beyond all estimation and equally valuable....The object offered on the altar...is Christ Himself, His Body and Blood, His holy Humanity (Dr. Nicolas Gihr, *The Holy Sacrifice of the Mass*, first published in German in 1877, English edition 1939, B. Herder Book Co., St. Louis, p. 135 – this book bore the official imprimatur of Archbishop Gleeson of St. Louis – emphasis added.)

If the person of the Redeemer had not yet been in the world, the priest by pronouncing the words of consecration, would produce this great person of a Man-God. "O wonderful dignity of the priests," cries out St. Augustine, "in their hands, as in the womb of the Blessed Virgin, the Son of God becomes incarnate." Hence the priests are called the parents of Jesus Christ....The priest may, in a certain manner, be called the creator of his Creator. "He that created me without me, is Himself created by me!" (Alphonsus de Liguori, *Dignity and Duties of the Priest*, Benziger Brothers Publishers, New York, 1888, pp. 32, 33).

Well may we see why Scripture declares,

And there was given unto him [the first beast of Revelation 13] a mouth speaking great things and blasphemies (Revelation 13:5).

No true Christian will deign to accept the Pope's indulgences, an indulgence God has never permitted him to offer. That is a usurpation of God's authority.

God has set out a salient fact — the majority will *not* be saved. This fact applies even when we confine our vision to Christians or to any one of the Christian sects. Let us remind ourselves of the indisputable words of Scripture.

The remnant shall return, even the remnant of Jacob, unto the mighty God. For though thy people Israel be as the sand of the sea, yet a remnant of them shall return: the consumption decreed shall overflow with righteousness (Isaiah 10:21,22).

This Old Testament prophecy was quoted by the apostle Paul and applied to the last days.

Esaias also crieth concerning Israel, Though the number of the children of Israel be as the sand of the sea, a remnant shall be saved: For he will finish the work, and cut it short in righteousness: because a short work will the Lord make upon the earth (Romans 9: 27,28).

Paul goes further and again quotes Isaiah who prophesied,

Except the Lord of hosts had left unto us a very small remnant, we should have been as Sodom, and we should have been like unto Gomorrah (Isaiah 1:9).

Paul's words were,

And as Esaias said before, Except the Lord of Sabaoth had left us a seed, we had been as Sodoma, and been made like unto Gomorrha (Romans 9:29).

The seed to which Paul refers is the "very small remnant."

It is this remnant of which Zephaniah prophesied of their character,

The remnant of Israel shall not do iniquity, nor speak lies; neither shall a deceitful tongue be found in their mouth: for they shall feed and lie down, and none shall make them afraid (Zephaniah 3:13).

While the Scripture speaks of much religious zeal in the end times in which we live, most of this will be unassociated with the character possessed by the remnant. Rather will most citizens be filled with the spirit of devils.

Now the Spirit speaketh expressly, that in the latter times some shall depart from the faith, giving heed to seducing spirits, and doctrines of devils (1 Timothy 4:1).

The religious will have experienced no real conversion but rather a facade or form of godliness only.

This know also, that in the last days perilous times shall come. For men shall be lovers of their own selves, covetous, boasters, proud, blasphemers, disobedient to parents, unthankful, unholy, Without natural affection, trucebreakers, false accusers, incontinent, fierce, despisers of those that are good, Traitors, heady, high-minded, lovers of pleasures more than lovers of God; Having a form of godliness, but denying the power thereof: from such turn away (2 Timothy 3:1-5).

Paul also wrote to Timothy describing an appalling spiritual declension amongst those who are churchgoers.

For the time will come when they will not endure sound doctrine; but after their own lusts shall they heap to themselves teachers, having itching ears; And they shall turn away their ears from the truth, and shall be turned unto fables (2 Timothy 4:3,4).

Such will no doubt go through the motions of religious observance when the prophesied dire natural disasters strike (Matthew 24:7) and even non-professors will comply with such requirements when severe penalties are imposed for noncompliance.

But Satan will not pour out his wrath upon those who are merely nominal in their Christian faith or who serve Him for matters of expediency or self-serving motives. Only those who, in God's grace and power, possess characters fitted for heaven and thus obey all His commandments including the Sabbath commandment, will feel the full fury of Satan implemented by those claiming to be doing the bidding of God. Then will be fulfilled Christ's prophecy:

They shall put you out of the synagogues: yea, the time cometh, that whosoever killeth you will think that he doeth God service (John 16:2).

Those receiving this wrath have been well described as the remnant.

And the dragon was wroth with the woman, and went to make war against the remnant of her seed, which keep the commandments of God, and have the testimony of Jesus Christ (Revelation 12: 17).

But the remnant will accept Christ's certain promise:

Be thou faithful unto death, and I will give thee a crown of life (Revelation 2:10).

For such martyrs, that price of heaven will be cheap enough.

BOOKS BY THE SAME AUTHORS

Antichrist is Here — This book challenges the concept that the Antichrist is a future being and demonstrates that Antichrist is present today. It is compelling and thought provoking reading.

Education for Excellence: The Christian Advantage — Both authors trained as elementary school teachers and taught for several years. Both have lectured at the university level, and Colin has been the president of three colleges. He is presently President of Hartland Institute which includes a college.

Family Crisis: God's Solution — Both authors have studied secular psychology. Colin has a Ph.D. and Russell, a first-class honors degree, in the discipline. But these concepts are discarded as the biblical principles of psychology and counseling are set forth.

Georgia Sits on Grandpa's Knee — A delightful children's storybook consisting of the experiences of Russell's children during their years of mission service in Southeast Asia.

Liberty in the Balance — This book traces the history of religious liberty in Europe and North America, and the lessons to be learned from it for today and the future.

Second Coming: Fervent Hope or Faded Dream — A survey of the powerful biblical evidence and details concerning Christ's second coming.

The Big Bang Exploded — This book demonstrates that evolution cannot possibly account for the founding of the universe and that creation alone centers on true aspects of science — biology, cosmology, and quantum physics. Both authors have studied science. Russell is a physician specializing in internal medicine.

The Evangelical Dilemma — Many doctrines of evangelical Protestantism are examined and evaluated by the Scripture. Both authors are ordained ministers of religion.

The Mystery of Death — The popular Christian view is challenged from Scripture, and its pagan roots exposed.

The Sacrificial Priest — A fascinating account of the sanctuary services and Christ's ministry, so crucial to our salvation, in the most holy place of the heavenly sanctuary.

You can find all these books and many more at

HARTLAND PUBLICATIONS
PO Box 1
Rapidan, VA 22733-0001

Order Line
1-800-774-3566